OPPORTUNITY OR PRIVILEGE:

Labor Legislation in America

Charles W. Baird

SP PC SOCIAL PHILOSOPHY & POLICY CENTER

ISBN 0-912051-02-7

5/11/87

Typesetting by   The Philosophy Documentation Center
                    Bowling Green State University

ACKNOWLEDGEMENTS

Thanks are due Morgan Reynolds, Texas A & M University; Dan Heldman, University of Dallas; John Kilgour, California State University, Hayward; and Henry Tombari, California State University, Hayward, for helpful suggestions and references.

Peggy Renk once again did a splendid typing job under pressure from an excessively impatient author.

Finally, my wife, Patti, tolerated yet another summer non-vacation in order that the manuscript could be completed on time. I promise to make up for it next year.

TABLE OF CONTENTS

Introduction

> The workers of America adhere to voluntary institutions in preference to compulsory systems which are held to be not only impractical but a menace to their rights, welfare and their liberty.
>
> Samuel Gompers
> *American Federationist*
> April 1916

The main theme of this book is that American unionism took a wrong turn with the passage of the National Labor Relations Act (the Wagner Act) in 1935. The NLRA substituted compulsion for voluntarism in the formation and operation of labor unions. Labor union leaders in power at the time supported the NLRA—indeed they twisted arms to get it passed. In doing so those labor union leaders betrayed the voluntarist ethic of Samuel Gompers, the first president of the American Federation of Labor. Moreover, and more importantly, they betrayed the principles of freedom of association and voluntary exchange so dear to the framers of the American Constitution. The fact that the United States Supreme Court upheld the constitutionality of the Wagner Act in *NLRB v. Jones & Laughlin Steel Corporation* (1937), following the infamous "switch in time that saved nine," says more about the political astuteness of the Court than the consistency of the Wagner Act with the Constitution.

In late June 1983 Pope John Paul II visited his native Poland. While there he proclaimed that humans have an "innate right" to freedom of association, and thus the right to form and join labor unions can never justly be denied. I fully agree with the Pope, and at the same time I hold that American unionism stands in violation of freedom of association and the innate rights of humans.

Another theme of this study is that what is conventionally believed about the history of the development of labor unions is untrue. There never was a long and bitter struggle between the owners of capital and people who make their living by selling labor services. Labor unions did not rescue sellers of labor from progressive impoverishment. Labor and capital are complementary, not competing, factors of production. The history of American unionism is one of conflicts between sellers of labor. Labor unions are simply cartels of sellers of labor services. They have always been chiefly concerned with suppressing competition in the selling of labor services. Like all cartels they face the problem of keeping competing sellers in line. Individualism and independence among workers is anathema to labor union leaders whose livelihood depends on membership dues and agency fees. The recognition strikes of the 1930's were simply struggles between workers who wanted to be independent and workers who wanted to cartelize. Public opinion was swayed in support of labor unions by falsely characterizing those struggles as contests between rich capitalists with huge bargaining power and poor workers with practically no bargaining power.

In what follows, I attempt to make these conclusions clear and convincing.

Chapter 1

The Philosophical and Analytical Framework

> What we learn from experience depends on the kind
> of philosophy we bring to experience. It is therefore
> useless to appeal to experience before we have set-
> tled, as well as we can, the philosophical question.
>
> C. S. Lewis
> *Miracles*
> 1947

The analyses and judgments in this book are based upon a particular philosophical perspective and a particular view of economics and economic systems. In this chapter that framework and some of its implications will be explained.

Natural Rights and Legislated Rights

While it is frequently asserted that people have such legislated rights as the right to housing, the right to a job, the right to a decent wage, the right to a good education, etc., such rights are not legitimate natural human rights. A person who asserts the existence of such rights is not using the word "rights" in the same sense as it was used by the authors of the United States Constitution. The American Founders wrote in the natural rights tradition of John Locke, the seventeenth century English political theorist. According to that tradition, a natural human right is one that grows out of the nature of man. Each person has such a right simply by virtue of the fact of being human. They are not entitlements granted to a person by government. They are, rather, rights inherent in being a person. A natural human right is inalienable. It can never justly be denied by any government, not even by majority rule.

It is a facet of human nature to attempt to achieve ends. All humans act purposively in pursuit of goals.[1] We do not all have the same goals, but we all attempt to achieve the goals we have. Now, when you undertake some action in pursuit of any of your goals you thereby implicitly assert that you have a right to do so. Having claimed this right for yourself you cannot, on pain of self contradiction, deny that other human beings also have the same right—to undertake action in pursuit of their goals.

If X is a legitimate natural human right, all people must possess X in exactly the same way. There can be no logical contradiction in the application of X to everyone at the same time. For example, the right to food is not a legitimate human right in the natural rights sense. If person A has a right to food in the sense that food will be made available to A no matter what A does, there must be some other person B who has the duty to provide the food to A. In that case, however, A and B do not have an equivalent right. A's alleged right to food imposes a duty to perform some positive act on B. If both A and B have a right to receive food, there must be some third person C who has the duty to provide the food. In that case C's right is different from that of A and B. It is logically impossible for all people to have a right to receive food no matter what they do because food must be provided by someone. Therefore, the right to food is not a natural right. All people do have a natural, food-related right—the right to make voluntary exchange offers to other individuals regarding food. Each person has a natural right to offer to buy, sell, give, or receive food on any terms he or she wishes. No person, however, has a natural right to force another to accept the offered terms. B can offer to give food to A at a zero price (or any price), but B cannot justly force A to accept the food at that price. A can offer to accept food from B for a zero price (or for any price), but A cannot justly force B to make the food available at that price.

Similarly no one has a natural right to a job. If person A has a right to a job in the sense that a job will be made available to A no matter what A does, there must be some other person B Who has the duty to provide the job to A. But if so, A and B do not have the same right. If A and B both have a right to a job in the sense that a job will be made available to each no matter what he does then there must be some third person C who has the duty to provide the jobs. In that case C's right is different from that of A and B. It is logically impossible for all people to have a right to a job no matter what they do because jobs must be provided by someone. Therefore the right to a job is not a natural right.

All people do have a natural job-related right—the right to make voluntary exchange offers regarding the purchase or sale of labor services at whatever terms one wishes. No person, however, has a natural right to force another to accept his or her offer.

When a duty to perform a positive act is imposed on one person by another, he or she loses some ability to pursue his or her own goals. Performing the duty uses time and resources that cannot then be used to pursue personal goals. When A pursues his goals in ways that impose duties on person B, A implicitly asserts that his goals have priority over B's goals. But if A's goals have priority over those of B, the reverse cannot also be true. A is claiming a right for himself in a way that denies the same right to B. The claimed right is not universal, therefore it is not a natural human right. When A claims the right to make voluntary exchange offers to B in the pursuit of his goals, he does not thereby implicitly deny that B has the same right. Since the right to make such offers can be simultaneously held and exercised by everyone, it meets the criterion of universal applicability.

A person's natural rights impose on others the duty to *refrain* from doing something. They impose a negative obligation on others. They impose the obligation to refrain from acts of coercion. This idea is often called the negative notion of freedom. Each person has a natural right to absence of coercion and interference from others. Today when most politicians and journalists talk about rights and freedom, they mean something quite different from the Founding Fathers. They talk about legislated rights. As we have seen, these rights often impose a burden on others to provide that to which the right is asserted. This is often called the positive notion of freedom. People should, according to this view, be free to acquire what they want even if that means that what is wanted must be taken from others.

Entitlements and Voluntary Exchange

In order for an exchange to be truly voluntary three criteria must be met: 1) each person must have a just entitlement to that which he or she offers in exchange or be acting as a fully authorized agent of a person who does have a just entitlement; 2) each person must have freely consented to consider the offers that are made; and 3) each person must be able to turn down offers without losing anything to which he or she is entitled. To what is a person justly entitled?[2] The basic axiom of natural rights theory is that each person is a self-owner. That is, you own your mental and physical abilities which constitute your human capital. It is a violation of natural law for one person to own another person. While the axiom of self-ownership is merely a normative assertion, it is one that enjoys widespread and general approval, at least in the Western World. In any event, John Locke began his argument with that axiom.

Labor is the service that a person performs using his or her human capital. If you own yourself you also own the labor that you perform using your human capital. If you own your own labor you, or a willing agent you designate, are the only ones who have a right to make voluntary exchange offers regarding that labor. If someone claims the right to represent you in bargaining for the sale of your labor services against your will, your natural rights have been violated.

The material world consists of people, gifts of nature, and things that have been produced by people mixing their labor with gifts of nature. According to Locke, a person acquires a just entitlement to unowned gifts of nature by being the first to mix his labor with the gift of nature in its natural, unowned state. The potter that uses clay from unowned land to make a pot owns the pot. He owns it because he owns the labor that created it. The labor transformed the land into something more serviceable to human wants. No one else has as good a claim to the pot as he whose labor created it. This idea is often called the labor theory of property. Property rights, or entitlements, to gifts of nature arise out of the mixing of owned labor with unowned land.

The labor theory of property is the direct basis for much land ownership in the United States. For example, in 1862 the Homestead Act was enacted. Under the Homestead Act a person could get private property rights to up to 160 acres of western land by living on the land and improving it (e.g., clearing, ploughing, planting) for five years. And so today, the labor theory of property is sometimes referred to as the home-stead principle.

One does not have to mix his own labor with a gift of nature in order to acquire a just entitlement thereto. A person who perceives the opportunity to create something using gifts of nature and then, by voluntary exchange contract, hires someone else to do the actual labor owns the resulting product. The person who provides the labor owns his own labor; but he has, by voluntary exchange contract, sold the use of the labor to the person who was alert to the creative opportunity. The act of creation came out of the alertness to the opportunity. Without that alertness and the subsequent hiring of the labor, nothing would have been made.[3]

Just entitlements can be justly transferred only by voluntary exchange. You can acquire a just entitlement to anything that someone else owns only if that person freely consents to the transfer of the entitlement. Perhaps the owner will consent to the transfer at a zero price, or perhaps he or she will insist on some positive price (in money or other goods and services) as a condition of voluntary transfer. Any arrangement that you both freely agree to that does not involve anyone else in any involuntary exchange is just.

If person A is forced to consider the offers B wants to make, the offers cannot properly be called voluntary exchange offers. Let's say that you are an electronics engineer and there is some computer company that wants to hire you. For whatever reason, you do not want to work for that company. If the company insists that you sit down and hear them out, you would probably feel righteously indignant. You would tell them to go away and not bother you. If they kept bothering you, you might even attempt to get the police to make them leave you alone. A voluntary interaction between two people must be voluntary on both sides. If you desire to be employed by the computer firm, but the firm is not interested in hiring you, you would have no natural right to force the firm to sit down and hear you out. If you claim the right to tell the firm to go away and not bother you, you must, on pain of self-contradiction, grant that the firm has the same right when it comes to deciding whether to bargain with you. Moreover, while you, and every other electronics engineer, have the right to designate any willing third party to act as your agent in the sale of labor services, the agent can receive from you only those rights that you had in the first place. Even if every electronics engineer freely designated the same willing third party to act as his agent, the agent would have no rights which were not possessed by the individual engineers. Thus, the computer company could, under natural law, tell the agent to go away and not bother it. Of course, if the agent represented all electrical engineers, the company would be unlikely to want to tell the agent to go away; but the company, nevertheless, would have a natural right to do so.

If you make a voluntary exchange offer to someone who rejects your offer you are entitled to seek out another person with whom to make and receive offers; i.e., with whom to bargain. If you are forbidden to seek out another voluntary exchange partner your natural rights are violated. If you make an offer to a group of people who, acting in concert, reject your offer, you are still entitled to seek out other voluntary exchange partners. Groups have only those rights which their individual members bring to them. The simple act of forming groups can create no new rights. Hence, there are no group rights which are different from individual rights.

The Nature of Government

In 1689 in his *Second Treatise of Government* John Locke set out his labor theory of property and explored the proper limits to which a government created out of social contract is subject. He said that the sole function of such a government is to protect the life, liberty, and property of its citizens. Any government that does not faithfully carry out this responsibility or tries to take advantage of its monopoly on the legal use of force to trespass against its citizens can justly be overthrown. Locke was writing in support of the British Glorious Revolution of 1688, but the American Founding Fathers put Locke's philosophy to good use in building their case against George III and in favor of the American Revolution of 1776.

The United States Constitution was written by people who drew their inspiration from the limited government, social contract theory of Locke. Proper government is limited to the provision of protective and judicial services. It has a monopoly on the legal use of force, but it cannot legitimately use that power to oppress its citizens. A government that goes beyond its proper limits loses its legitimacy, for it joins the ranks of the predators it was originally designed to resist. Government should do no more than enforce the proscription on involuntary exchange. As F. A. Hayek puts it, government exists only to enforce the universal rules of just conduct.[4] Just conduct between people is limited to voluntary exchange.

The fact that government has a monopoly of the legal use of force presents a temptation to those who wield governmental power to use it for their own ends, contrary to the will of those they govern. Some means had to be found to provide the governed with some measure of control over government. The means that emerged out of the British experience of the seventeenth century and was adopted by the American Founders was political democracy. Those who wield governmental power were to be chosen according to majority rule voting procedures. Governmental officials so chosen would make rules and laws by majority rule voting among themselves.

Majority rule voting, wherein those in the minority are bound by the will of the majority, was devised as a check on governmental abuse of its monopoly on the legal use of force. There is absolutely nothing in the historical record of the evolution of political democracy that suggests that forcing a minority to submit to the will of a majority is proper except in the election of those who wield governmental power and in the decision-making procedures that those so-elected must use. Coercion is reprehensible. It should be avoided whenever possible. When a minority is bound by the will of a majority the minority is coerced. Hence, mandatory submission to majority rule voting cannot be justified on its own merits. It is justified in the case of governmental decision-making not because it is good and desirable in and of itself, but because it is the only way we know of to give those who are governed some control over government. There cannot be one government for the majority and others for various minorities. Government by its very nature must have a monopoly on the legal use of force. Since there can only be one government in any geographical area, majority rule must be employed.

However, this does not mean that anything that a majority wants government to do is justified. Proper government is limited government. Mandatory submission to the will of a majority is justifiable only in those matters over which governmental power properly extends. The United States Supreme Court expressed this idea very clearly in *West Virginia State Board of Education v. Barnette:*

> The very purpose of the Bill of Rights was to withdraw certain subjects from the vicissitudes of political controversy, to place them beyond the reach of majorities.... One's...fundamental rights may not be submitted to vote; they depend on the outcome of no elections.[5]

If a majority wants government to execute Catholics, it is *not* proper to execute Catholics. If a majority wants government to steal the property of Jews and give it to members of the Ku Klux Klan, it is *not* proper to do so. Likewise, if a majority wants government to take property away from people with high incomes and give it to people with low incomes, it is *not* proper to do so.

If the last sentence seems wrong, ask yourself what is the substantive difference between the last two sentences. If it is morally wrong for the law to discriminate against people based on religion, then it is, also, morally wrong for the government to discriminate against people on the basis of income and wealth. A government bound by natural law is bound to treat all cititzens exactly alike. Taking something from A and giving it to B is to treat A and B in a fundamentally different way.

It is often said that the United States has a government of laws and not of men. The Founders intended that such would be the case. To them a government of laws was a government bound by natural law. No piece of legislation which was contrary to natural law would be acceptable. Today, however, many politicians and journalists mean something entirely different when they refer to a government of laws rather than of men. They mean that all men must obey whatever laws the government passes as long as they were passed following correct procedures. Whether the substantive content of the laws is consistent with natural law is, to them, entirely irrelevant. Despite what the Supreme Court said in the *Barnette* case quoted above, it too has adopted this attitude in cases involving property rights. And they have done so despite the fact that the Fifth and Fourteenth Amendments guarantee that government will protect the life, liberty, and property of its citizens. More will be said about this in the next chapter.

The Market Process

Bad ideas have bad consequences. One particularly bad idea, with especially bad consequences, is that capital and labor have been and continue to be locked in a struggle with each other. Karl Marx constructed a theory of historical determinism based solely on the idea of this alleged struggle. The American labor union movement thrives on the belief that capital and labor are natural enemies. Labor, in this mythology, is inherently weak. Workers must band together if they are to have any chance of effectively fighting the owners of captial for their fair share of the economic pie. Folk singers such as Pete Seeger propagated the class struggle myth, depicting the owners of capital as profit-thirsty villains constantly resisting the efforts of workers to get their fair share. The idea of the long and bitter struggle by workers to secure economic justice through labor unions is so engrained in the American ethos that anyone who calls the idea into question runs the risk of being dismissed out of hand. Nevertheless, the only effective remedy for bad ideas is better ideas. Let's consider what the relationship between people who make their living selling the services of their human capital (i.e., selling their labor), and people who make their living selling the services of their nonhuman capital really is.

In a voluntary exchange economic system there are essentially two types of markets—input markets and output markets.[6] In each market there are buyers and sellers. Inputs, often called productive resources, are labor, the services of nonhuman capital (e.g., machinery, buildings, and tools), and the services of land (e.g., raw materials). People are owners of these resources. Each person owns his or her own labor, some people own (nonhuman) capital, and still others own land. The sellers in the input market, then, are the owners of the productive resources.

The buyers in the input market are people called entrepreneurs. A successful entrepreneur is a person who is alert to situations where it is possible to assemble resources by voluntary exchange contracts with resource owners for a total cost that is less than what buyers are willing to pay for the resulting product. The key characteristic of an entrepreneur is his or her alertness to such opportunities to make profit. If buyers are willing to pay more for a product or service than the payments that the entrepreneur must make to the owners of the resources that must be assembled in order to produce the product or service, then there is something left over for the entrepreneur. The desire for that residual—that *profit*—is what motivates the entrepreneur to attempt to identify such opportunities. The consequence of such entrepreneurial alertness is that resources are constantly being redirected toward uses that buyers value more highly and away from uses that buyers value less highly.

We call those who sell their labor services to entrepreneurs *workers*, and we call those who sell the services of the capital they own to entrepreneurs *capitalists*. A capitalist is merely a resource owner. He or she owns nonhuman capital the services of which are useful in the production of goods and services. Henry Ford was a capitalist because he owned much nonhuman capital. He was also an entrepreneur because he assembled capital, from himself and others, together with labor services and raw materials from still others in order to produce automobiles. Anyone can be an entrepreneur—a capitalist, a worker, as well as a land owner. Some entrepreneurs have no resources at all except their alertness to profit opportunities.

Entrepreneurs are the essential productive force in any voluntary exchange economy. Resource owners, as resource owners, merely compare the price offers that different entrepreneurs bid for their resources. Each resource owner tries to sell his resources to the highest bidder. It is the entrepreneurs who pay attention to what buyers of final products and services want and how keenly they want it. On the basis of those perceptions, entrepreneurs decide how much they can bid for the use of resources. If final buyers place a low value on product X, entrepreneurs will have to put in low bids for resources to produce X. If those bids are lower than what the resource owners can get from other entrepreneurs who are attempting to assemble resources for the production of other products, X will not be produced. This is why it is incorrect to say that costs determine prices. In fact it is the other way around. Prices (what final product buyers are ready, willing, and able to pay) determine costs (the payments made by entrepreneurs to resource owners). Entrepreneurs are buyers in input markets and sellers in output markets. Entrepreneurs are the links between the two types of markets.

Entrepreneurs do not always make a profit, but they always strive to make a profit. Sometimes they think buyers are willing and able to pay more than the buyers are actually willing and able to pay. On the basis of that error, such entrepreneurs then bid more for resources than they recover when they sell the final product or service to buyers. This means that they incur losses.

Entrepreneurs who make profits want to increase production and other entrepreneurs imitate them, so more of those profitable products and services will be produced. Entrepreneurs who suffer losses seek out other products and services to produce so less of the unprofitable products and services are produced. Entrepreneurial profit-seeking and loss-avoiding behavior steers resource deployment toward those things of which buyers want more and away from those things of which buyers want less. The pattern of resource deployment is not constant. It must constantly change to keep up with the constantly changing wants of buyers.

Capitalists, on the other hand, do not make profit. Economists call the payments that entrepreneurs make to capitalists *interest*. Payments that entrepreneurs make to sellers of labor services are called *wages* and *salaries*. *Profit* is merely a residual that a successful entrepreneur gets to keep, and *losses* are a burden that unsuccessful entrepreneurs must bear. Capitalists, workers, and landowners are all contractual claimants on what the entrepreneur receives from final product buyers. The entrepreneur assembles resources for production by entering into hiring contracts with resource owners. The resource payments are specified in those contracts. The entrepreneur is the residual claimant. It is he who keeps what is left over, if anything is left over. It is he who bears the losses that arise from errors. It is he who is the risk bearer.

When an entrepreneur correctly perceives a profit opportunity, his success will be imitated. Other entrepreneurs will enter the market and bid for resources to produce the same product or service. Thus, payments to resource owners will increase. When these second generation entrepreneurs, the imitators, then attempt to sell what they produce, they make competing offers to consumers which will mean that the prices buyers will pay will decrease. In this way entrepreneurial profit from the production of any particular product will erode until the amount collected from buyers is just enough to meet the contractual claims of the resource owners. If the entrepreneur is hiring some capital from himself—i.e., if the entrepreneur is also acting as a capitalist—he will then just be making a normal return, a normal interest, from his business. He may continue this for some time, or he may leave the operation of this mature business to someone else and venture off on a quest for more profit from a new, riskier venture.

This *market-process-view* of profit, what it is and what it does, is quite different from the image of profit created by those who have a vested interest in the mythological struggle between owners of capital and workers. The market process view implies that profit is a friend of labor as well as a friend of all resource owners and, indeed, of all consumers. The existence of profit leads to competitive entrepreneurial bidding for resources which, in turn, results in higher payments to resource owners. Profit is also a friend of final product buyers. The existence of profit leads to competitive selling of finished products and services in output markets which, in turn, leads to lower product and services prices. The entrepreneur's desire for profit is what assures buyers that the pattern of production will constantly be revised in attempts to keep up with the ever-changing pattern of what people want. Production for profit is production for use.

The market-process-view stresses that labor and the services of capital are complementary, not competing, productive resources. Labor alone produces nothing. Capital alone produces nothing. Labor and capital together without entrepreneurs produce nothing. Entrepreneurs identify what they think are profitable production opportunitites and then employ capital and labor together with raw materials and supplies to sieze the opportunities. Production is a team effort with the success of the team depending on all of the parts. The Japanese have never lost sight of this vital insight. Today, they are effectively exploiting it to out-compete American producers in many fields.

The Labor Market

According to the 1914 Clayton Act, about which more will be said in the next chapter, "the labor of a human being is not a commodity or article of commerce." This assertion was made in an attempt to justify exempting labor unions from the 1890 Sherman Antitrust Act, but the assertion is utter nonsense. An article of commerce is simply something that is bought and sold. It is true that a person is not an article of commerce, but a person's labor is not the person. A person's labor is the service that he or she performs using his or her mental and physical abilities. Services performed by people are bought and sold every day. The services of union leaders are bought and sold, as are the services of teachers, doctors, lawyers, and candlestick makers. As such those services are articles of commerce.

Labor services are measured in units called labor hours. The price of one labor hour is called the wage rate. (If a person receives a salary, it can always be expressed on a per hour basis.) There is an upper limit to what an employer is willing to pay for one unit of labor services from any particular worker. The upper limit, what economists call the employer's demand price for the unit of labor service, depends on what the employer perceives the unit of labor service can do for him. Labor services are employed along with other productive resources to produce a product or service which in turn is sold to customers. The significance of a unit of labor time depends on how much more of the product is produced when an additional hour of labor time is used than would be produced if an additional labor hour were not employed, and it also depends on how much money the additional output will bring into the firm when it is sold. The additional revenue that is brought into the firm from the sale of the additional output that is produced when an additional unit of labor is employed is called the *marginal revenue product* of that labor. The employer's demand price for one unit of that labor is that unit's marginal revenue product.

There is a lower limit to the wage that a worker will accept for an hour of his labor time. This lower limit is called the *worker's supply price* for an hour of his labor time, and it depends on the value that the worker attaches to the most highly-valued alternative use of his time available to him. If McDonalds offers $3.50 per hour to a student for a summer job, that student will decline the offer if his supply price is greater than $3.50 per hour. The supply price may, for example, be $4.00 per hour because there is some alternative employment opportunity that offers $4.00 per hour. It also may be $4.00 per hour because this student places that much value on each hour of summertime leisure. The crucial point is that a person's supply price depends on what that person's alternatives are. The less attractive the alternative uses of time, the lower will be that person's supply price for an hour of his or her labor in any particular employment.

So there is an upper limit to what an employer is willing to pay for an hour of a person's time based on the significance (in money terms) to the employer of the use of that hour of labor, and there is a lower limit to what a person will accept as a condition for agreeing to work for an hour for any employer which depends on the values the person attaches to alternative uses of the time. What determines the wage that a person will actually receive in any particular employment in an unrestricted labor market is the extent of two kinds of competition—competition between employers to hire workers, and competition between workers who do the same kind of work to secure employment. For a given number of people offering to sell a particular labor service, the larger the number of employers who are attempting to hire that type of labor, the higher the wage that will be paid. For a given number of employers attempting to hire a particular type of labor, the larger the number of people attempting to find employment doing that type of labor the lower will be the wage paid.

An employer is willing to pay up to his or her demand price for an hour of your labor. The employer is delighted if he can get away with paying less than his demand price. Different employers are likely to have different demand prices. Suppose employer A's demand price is $10 per hour, and employer B's demand price is $6 per hour. If there are no other employers for whom you could work, the lowest price you could receive for working for employer A is $6. This is because it is profitable for Employer B to hire you at any wage less than or equal to $6, and you would not work for employer A unless A's offer was at least as good as B's offer. Of course, if employer A is the only employer for whom you could work (a situation economists call monopsony), the lowest wage you could receive in an unrestricted labor market would be the value you attach to your use of leisure time. Similarly if employers A and B collude together to offer you only $4 per hour, and if $4 per hour is above your supply price, that is the wage you will be paid. In general, in an unrestricted market, no person will for long be paid a wage in his job that is less than his marginal revenue product in his next best employment opportunity. Active competition between employers to secure the services of employees for wages less than those employees' marginal revenue products assures that result.

Of course employees' knowledge of alternative employment opportunities and employers' knowledge of characteristics of potential employees is imperfect. Adjustments to changing conditions in the labor market are never instantaneous. But we know that in time such adjustments always tend to be made. We know that, surely, because it is profitable for employers and employees alike to seek out better terms of trade.

Bargaining Power

As we just saw, competition that determines what a person's wage will be in an unrestricted market is of two kinds—between employees and between employers. Employees compete with each other to secure jobs providing attractive wages and benefits. Employers compete with each other to secure the services of employees for wages less than those employees' marginal revenue products. Employees and employers do not compete with each other because they are on opposite sides of the market. They do not compete with each other, but they do bargain with each other.

In any voluntary exchange between two people both people expect to gain. A worker accepts a job offer from a particular employer if and only if that offer exceeds the worker's supply price. The employer purchases the services of a particular employee if and only if the wage paid is less than the employer's demand price. At any wage greater than the worker's supply price and, also, less than the employer's demand price, both gain from the hiring contract. The employer wants to pay as little as possible, but both are constrained. The employer cannot obtain the services of the employee for less than the employee's supply price, and the employee cannot receive for the job more than the employer's demand price. They must bargain to determine the actual wage paid. The employer has strong bargaining power if there are no (or few) alternative employers for whom the potential employee can work and if there are several other people available to take the job. The employee has strong bargaining power if there are several other employers for whom he could work and if there are not many other people available to take the job. The bargaining power of each, in other words, depends on competition between employees for the employment and competition between employers to secure the labor services of workers.

Cartels

A cartel is an agreement among otherwise independent sellers of a product or service to act together, rather than competitively, in their selling efforts. It is an arrangement whereby competition between the sellers is suppressed and a united front is presented to buyers. Buyers are confronted with a stated price (or other terms) which no individual seller will undercut. Buyers are, in effect, confronted with only one seller. If all independent sellers have joined the cartel, there are no alternative sellers from whom the buyers can buy that particular product. Competition has been replaced by monopoly. Some cartels are illegal and some others are legal in the United States. For example, when in the 1950s the manufacturers of electric generators conspired to quash competition among themselves and all charge the same price while dividing up the market, the officers of those firms were prosecuted, and some even went to jail. On the other hand, labor unions are legal cartels. All the sellers of labor services to the automobile industry have (some willingly, and some not so willingly) joined together into the United Automobile Workers Union. Acting together they fix the price for the labor they sell. No individual workers would dare undercut the fixed wage.

In an unrestricted market cartels do not survive for very long. If the cartel is unsupported by government legislation, its members will soon begin to compete with each other, and the cartel will gradually disintegrate. There are three main reasons why this is so. First, *not all members of a cartel have identical interests*. What is optimal for some of them may not be optimal for others. The first problem a cartel must solve is securing agreement among its members about what prices and other terms of trade to attempt to set up. Many cartels have floundered right at the outset because of fighting among their members about what prices and quotas to fix. Second, once an agreement has been reached among the cartel members, it is always in the interest of any one individual member to cheat on the rules. If all other members stick to the rules and do not act competitively while one does act competitively, that one will get some additional income above what he would get if he stuck to the rules. The cheater would be acting as a free-rider on the noncompetitive activity of his fellows. If they don't counter his efforts with competitive actions of their own, the cheater meets no resistance as he cuts price and gives special considerations under the table to enlarge his share of the market. Every member of a cartel is subject to the temptation to become such a free-rider, and every member of the cartel is afraid that if he does not cheat someone else will begin to cheat and then, in self-defense, others will join in. The cartel collapses, and competition is restored. Economists call this second problem *the free-rider problem*. Third, if a cartel is set up and begins to act successfully, temporarily overcoming the free-rider problem, it will generate above normal (above competitive) profit rates for the group, which it then divides up among its members. *These high profit rates will attract outside entrepreneurs into the market*. As these newcomers assemble resources and begin to sell in the market, competition returns. Members begin to panic and act competitively to attempt to protect their turf from the newcomers. Perhaps, the newcomers can be brought into the cartel. But if so, the group gets bigger and more difficult to manage. The probability that some will fall prey to the free-rider temptation then increases.

The only way that cartels have ever been able to endure is to enlist the power of government on their side. If the government will pass laws which block newcomers from entering the market, which punish individual sellers who cut price or otherwise act competitively, and which declare what the rules of the cartel will be, all of the cartel's problems will vanish. This is what the federal government has done in many cases. The Interstate Commerce Commission was explicitly set up to overcome the inability of the railroads to set up a workable cartel on their own. Ditto for the Civil Aeronautics Board in the case of airlines. As we shall see, the Wagner Act did precisely the same thing for labor unions.

NOTES

1. In economics this is called the action axiom. For a complete discussion of this axiom and its logical implications see Ludwig von Mises, *Human Action*, (New Haven: Yale University Press, 1949).

2. The answers given here are from Robert Nozick, *Anarchy, State and Utopia*, (New York: Basic Books, 1974), Part II. Nozick's theory of entitlements is based on the property

rights theory of John Locke (1632-1704). For an excellent discussion of Locke see Karen I. Vaughn, "John Locke's Theory of Property: Problems of Interpretation," *Literature of Liberty* , Spring 1980, pp. 5-37.

3. Israel Kirzner, "Entrepreneurship, Entitlement, and Economic Justice," in *Perception, Opportunity and Profit*, (Chicago: University of Chicago Press, 1979), Chapter 12.

4. F. A. Hayek, *Law Legislation and Liberty*, Vol. I, *Rules and Order* (Chicago: University of Chicago Press, 1973).

5. 319 U. S. 624 (1943).

6. What follows is based on Israel Kirzner, *Competition and Entrepreneurship*, (Chicago: University of Chicago Press, 1973).

Chapter 2

Some Labor Union History

> Historical myths have perhaps played nearly as great a role in shaping opinion as historical facts. Yet we can hardly hope to profit from past experience unless the facts from which we draw our conclusions are correct.
>
> F. A. Hayek
> *Capitalism and the Historians*
> 1954

If the proverbial man on the street was asked what he thinks of labor unions today he would most likely say something like: "Labor unions were needed at one time, and they have done a lot of good; lately however they have become a problem." In my judgment, however, the type of labor unions we now have were never needed, and they never did any good for anyone except some of their members and most of their leaders. Those who gained did so at the expense of other workers, not at the expense of employers. The common acceptance of American-style labor unions as a legitimate institution arises from beliefs based upon myths and confusions about how free markets operate.

The Myths

A few years ago I was asked to review six world history textbooks that were in common use in the high school market. I focused on the quality of the economics lessons that they explicitly or implicitly taught. The standard treatment of the industrial revolution in these books depicts it as a horrible experience for everyone but the capitalist owners of the factories. Working hours, working conditions, wages, and safety were dreadful.

Wealth, to be sure, was created, but it went mostly to capitalists while the workers' lot worsened. These texts alleged that it took labor unions and factory legislation to turn the industrial revolution into an engine of progress for everyone, rather than a means for the aggrandizement of the capitalist elite.

This vision of the industrial revolution and the condition of working people is extremely widespread. Many people have a romantic notion that life prior to the industrial revolution and the capitalist era was idyllic. The image many people carry around in their heads about life before capitalism is one of blue skies, soft billowy clouds, open fields richly decorated with brightly colored flowers and peaceful animals, and pretty cottages kept warm by sunshine during the day and glowing embers in quaint fireplaces at night. Children, leading care-free healthy lives, gamboled through the fields while their mothers kept a watchful eye, even while preparing healthy meals for the family to enjoy as the sun set.

Then came the capitalists. Clouds were replaced with smoke as the factories darkened the sky and despoiled the countryside. Men, women, and children were herded into "dark Satanic mills" (as William Blake expressed it) in which life, limb, and health were put in jeopardy in the service of the villianous capitalists who cared about nothing but profit.

The conditions that supposedly existed during the industrial revolution precipitated the need for labor unions. In the unfettered, "capitalist" system (Marx's pejorative expression for a private property, voluntary exchange economic system) workers have no alternative but to submit to the oppression of the capitalist class. Workers are, on their own, incapable of sharing in the goods and services that their labor creates. This can only be remedied, these high school textbooks assert, by enlightened social legislation and the formation of labor unions.

Other commonly-held beliefs passed down by folk singers, popular writers, clergy, academics, and the press include the following:

In an unrestricted market workers necessarily have less bargaining power than employers. Unionization is the only way that this imbalance in bargaining power can be redressed. Workers must join together to acquire bargaining power before they can force concessions from capitalists.

In America during the nineteenth and early twentieth centuries governments in general and courts in particular acted at the behest of employers to suppress unionization. Courts applied the common law doctrine of criminal conspiracy to smash the legitimate organizing efforts of hapless workers. When a union was able to get organized and call a strike, government rescued the employer with injunctions forbidding the union to carry out what were perfectly just actions. If the injunction didn't work, then the police and even troops would be sent in to break the strike.

The 1894 Pullman strike is a favorite story. A typical, pro-union account of the Pullman strike, which illustrates the above point, can be found in a widely-used high school American history textbook (not one of those alluded to earlier).

A famous case of federal intervention occured near Chicago in 1894 when a strike was called against the Pullman Palace Car Company by the American Railway Union led by Eugene V. Debs. The strike was supported by railway workers around Chicago and elsewhere, who refused to handle trains which included Pullman cars. When Governor Altgeld of Illinois refused to call out the state militia or ask for federal help, President Cleveland sent federal troops anyway. Cleveland declared that such action was justified in order to guarantee mail delivery, although mail trains were in fact running and the mails were being delivered....

In the late 1800s the courts no less than governors and Presidents, generally used their powers in behalf of management. For example, during the Pullman strike the railroad owners asked a federal court in Chicago to issue an injunction, or court order, forbidding Debs and other labor leaders to continue the strike. The court issued the injunction. It justified this action on the ground that the strikers had entered into "a conspiracy in restraint of trade" and were therefore violating the Sherman Antitrust Act of 1890, which declared such conspiracies illegal.

Debs defied the court order. He was promptly arrested, and sentenced to six months in jail for refusing to obey the injunction. Labor denounced this conviction as "government by injunction." But the Supreme Court in 1895 upheld the ruling, Debs was jailed, and the strike was broken.[1]

According to union mythology, a favorite device of extortion used by employers was called the yellow dog contract. In order to secure a job to feed himself and his family a worker had to sign an agreement with the employer whereby the employee promised never to join, support, or have anything else to do with a labor union. The courts, even the Supreme Court, in, for example, *Adair v. U. S.* (1908) participated in this travesty of justice by enforcing these yellow dog contracts.

Railroad workers were the first to receive proper support from government in the Railway Labor Act of 1926. But other workers continued to be frustrated in their attempts to organize.

Then came the Great Depression of the 1930s. It was clear to everyone that capitalism had failed. Free markets and voluntary exchange led to disaster. People finally came to see the truth of what labor leaders and other socially concerned people had claimed all along: government must intervene in the labor market and, indeed, in all markets if rational order was to be restored and maintained. The miserably low wages paid to workers played a major role in generating the depression. With low wages workers couldn't buy the goods and services that were produced. Those goods and services accumulated, and production cutbacks with their concomitant layoffs ensued. Wages must be raised to cure the depression, and the best way to raise wages was through unionization.

In 1932 a measure of relief was received with the passage of the Norris-LaGuardia Act which made yellow dog contracts unenforceable in federal courts and greatly restricted the use of injunctions to break strikes. Franklin Roosevelt was elected in 1932 and in 1933 Section 7(a) of the National Industrial Recovery Act finally granted long-denied, fundamental rights to organize to most workers.

But employers continued to thwart the legitimate hopes of workers and the desires of the new President and Congress by the formation of company unions which employers falsely claimed met the requirements of Section 7(a). Recognition strikes were called in order to try to get employers to recognize true unions rather than their own company unions. Much strife and conflict ensued as employers refused to recognize any of the independent unions and forced their employees to become members of company unions.

To make matters worse, in May 1935 the Supreme Court declared that the National Industrial Recovery Act was unconstitutional. This left workers with no protection at all against rapacious employers. But President Roosevelt and Senator Robert Wagner (D, NY) got the Congress to pass the Wagner Act later in July 1935. The Wagner Act finally gave workers all of the rights they deserved but had, for so long, been denied. In April 1937 the Supreme Court said the Wagner Act was constitutional, and rational order was finally applied to labor relations. The constant strife that all employees had suffered in the labor market was the result of workers being denied their rights. Now that the law guaranteed those rights labor peace would reign.

There we have it. That is, in broad outline, what most people seem to believe about the history of labor and labor unions up to the enactment of the Wagner Act. In the next section I will examine many of these beliefs and show them to be questionable at best. W. H. Hutt has nicely summarized these beliefs and their effects in this way:

The genuineness of many of the influential and disinterested leaders of thought and opinion who have faith in the story of "labor's bitter struggle" against oppression is enormously important. For instance in the United States, when the Norris-LaGuardia and the Wagner acts were being passed, the public opinion to which Congress is sensitive reflected the conviction that, in the past, "labor" had been shamefully treated. Time-honored but virtually fictional stories of the inequities and iniquities of former days had been propagated and reiterated with conviction by public-spirited novelists, journalists, clergymen, and academics, as well as by parties seeking to exploit the myths. And the American labor legislation of the 1930s was endorsed, it seems to me, by people who simply wanted to turn the tables.... All of the old injustices, inequalities and exploitation were to be swept away. The power of "the employers" to oppress their workers was to be ended and an age of economic justice was to be ushered in. Few economists in the United States who perceived the folly of the legislative steps then being taken could conceive of any effective manner in which to communicate their warnings....

The Norris-LaGuardia and Wagner acts will, I predict, come to be regarded by future historians as economic blunders of the first magnitude.[2]

Setting the Record Straight

In this section I critically consider the six common beliefs adumbrated above. In the final two sections of this chapter, I examine the legislative history leading up to the Wagner Act and the actual nature of the recognition strikes of the early 1930s.

1. The Industrial Revolution

The facts of the industrial revolution are well outlined in *Capitalism and the Historians* edited by F. A. Hayek.[3] Real wages in England, where the industrial revolution began, fell from 1780 to 1800 (mainly due to the enclosure movement in agriculture which freed large amounts of labor from agricultural employment and made it available for industrial employment while at the same time increasing agricultural production), but then increased substantially almost without interruption throughout the rest of the 19th Century.

Figure 2-1 shows what happened to real wages in England in the period 1780-1880. The real wages are represented as an index with 1780=100.

Figure 2-1

Real Wages in England, 1780-1880

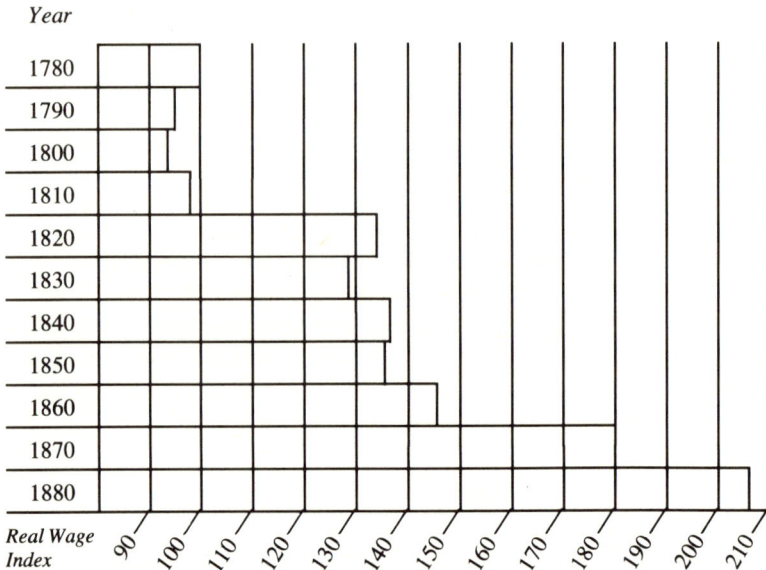

Year

Year	Real Wage Index

Chart axis — Year: 1780, 1790, 1800, 1810, 1820, 1830, 1840, 1850, 1860, 1870, 1880

Real Wage Index: 90, 100, 110, 120, 130, 140, 150, 160, 170, 180, 190, 200, 210

Source: John M. Thompson & Kathleen Hedberg, *People and Civilizations* (Lexington, MA: Ginn & Co., 1977), p. 552

In other words, the benefits of the industrial revolution were not received only by factory owners. Workers also received substantial improvements in their command over goods and services. Moreover, these improvements were obtained long before there was any substantial formation of unions or implementation of factory legislation.

Economic theory predicts this result because increased industrialization increases both the maximum amount an employer is willing to pay for a worker's services and the extent of competition among employers for workers' services.

Of course, in order for this rivalry to be effective in raising wages it is necessary for workers and employers to become aware of their available alternatives and to be able and willing to move to take advantage of them. This suggests that real wages should increase as improvements in transportation and communication become available. It was precisely the industrial revolution that established such improvements.

As we look back from today's vantage point at working conditions, living conditions, and wages from 1780 to 1900 (the dates most commonly given to delimit the industrial revolution) we recoil in horror at what we see. The point that is most forcefully made in the Hayek book is that relative to what workers had to put up with before the industrial revolution, conditions and wages during the industrial revolution were attractive. To be sure, women and children worked long, tedious, and dangerous hours in the factories for little pay. Without the factories they would have worked long, tedious, and dangerous hours on manors for even less pay. Or they would have been dead. Only when industrializaton, and therefore the productivity of labor, had progressed far enough so that a whole family could be supported by the labor services of only one worker would it be possible for many women and children to devote their time to activities other than selling labor services. But for this to occur civilization would have to await the full flowering of the industrial revolution.

Population soared during the industrial revolution although the birth rate changed little. Most of the population gains were due to declining death rates. This doesn't square too well with the common notion in most history books that sanitary and general living conditions deteriorated during the industrial revolution. To be sure, many of the factory cities had crowded slums with open sewers and dark houses. The taxes that the British government imposed on windows and the use of bricks goes a long way to account for the lack of sewers and windows. Even then living conditions were an improvement over what the lower classes accepted as normal prior to the industrial revolution.

Most of the evidence upon which myths of the industrial revolution are based is anecdotal rather than statistical. Mr. and Mrs. J. L. Hammonds' books are frequently quoted to support the myths, but in 1934 the Hammonds candidly admitted:

> Statisticians tell us that when they have put in order such data as they can find, they are satisfied that earnings increased and that most men and women were less poor when this discontent was loud and active then they were when the eighteenth century was beginning to grow old in a silence like that of autumn. The evidence, of course, is scanty, and its interpretaion not too simple, but this general view is probably more or less correct.[4]

The simple truth is that the industrial revolution was a blessing for the common man, and this was true long before unionism or social legislation could have had any effect.

2. *Bargaining Power*

During the early 1930s up to the passage of the Wagner Act much was made of the common belief that workers necessarily had less bargaining power than employers. Everyone simply knew that employers always had many potential employees they could hire. Employers could simply take their pick, playing one worker off against another to get the wage rate as low as possible. Employees, on the other hand, were always in a take-it-or-leave-it situation. They either worked for the employer with whom they were bargaining at the moment or they didn't work.

In Chapter 1 we saw that an employee's bargaining power depends on the number of employers for whom he could work and the number of other workers seeking the same kind of employment. Looking back on the late nineteenth century through the first three decades of the twentieth century we see a period of substantial economic growth. The number of jobs available more than kept up with the growth in the active labor force. The automobile and other communication devices greatly expanded the geographic scope of workers' job searches. No longer were workers forced to seek employment from a small number of employers in their home towns. They could seek employment in the next town, the next state, or all over the country. This one fact more than anything else increased competition in the labor market in favor of workers, and, therefore, increased workers' bargaining power.

Irving Bernstein, a highly respected economic historian of the New Deal period, and one who is a strong labor union supporter, wrote this about the status of labor during the 1920s to 1932:

> Postwar prosperity with its rising standard of living and materialism nurtured individualistic rather than concerted tendencies among workers. Even those who remained (union) members were apathetic.... Prosperous workers identified themselves socially with the middle class, engaging in emulative spending and sending their children to college. They came to believe they were "getting ahead" and that there was a place for them or their progeny in an expanding future.... New devices, the automobile, the radio, and the movies, absorbed their time and scattered their interests with a consequent sapping of the vitality of unionism. One organizer declared that "the Ford car has done a lot of harm to the unions." Since unions contributed little to their improved status, workers saw no point in joining.[5]

This does not suggest that workers were suffering from a lack of bargaining power. It depicts a labor market in which the competition among employers to secure the services of workers was increasing the prosperity of almost everyone involved.

The bargaining power argument, however, was not used very much prior to the Great Depression. In fact, there was not very much competition between employers to hire labor during most of the depression. But that by itself would not imply that employers had a bargaining power advantage over employees. Both groups were in bad shape. Employers who did seek to hire workers had to lower the wages they offered to workers because their customers were lowering their expenditures on goods and services. Competition between employers to sell their goods and services gave them little bargaining power. Later in this section we will consider the causes of the Great Depression. Here the point is that to the extent employees lost bargaining power during that period, so too did employers.

With the passage of the National Industrial Recovery Act (NIRA) in June 1933 things changed. Under this Act manufacturers were permitted to cartelize without fear of prosecution under the antitrust laws. Manufacturers in each market were told to meet together and negotiate industry codes that would fix prices and other terms of trade in each industry. Once a code was adopted in an industry it would be illegal for any seller to cut his price below the official price or to violate any other proscription of competition embodied in the code. The federal government would prosecute any violations. And, indeed, violators were prosecuted. Sellers of many things, including milk and chickens, were hauled before the courts for having the temerity to cut the price they charged when they offered to sell things that they themselves owned.

Now that employers were encouraged, even ordered, by government to join together in cartels rather than compete, employers did acquire some bargaining power advantage over employees. No longer would employers compete for labor. They would get together, with government's blessing, and fix wages they would offer. Clearly, this put workers at a disadvantage relative to employers in wage bargainng. Labor union leaders and sympathizers quickly seized the opportunity to advocate compulsory unionism as the obvious remedy to the imbalance. The declaration of policy in Section 1 of the 1935 Wagner Act explicitly asserted that one of the purposes of the bill was to redress the imbalance of bargaining power caused by the organization of employers.[6] In evaluating the arguments pro and con for the Wagner Act, Irving Bernstein wrote:

> Employers were free to form partnerships, corporations, and associations which had among their purposes the conduct of relationships with employees.

> The case in which workers or unions denied employers the right so to associate was virtually nonexistent...on the other hand, employers frequently intervened to deny correlative rights to their employees.[7]

Bernstein concluded that the Wagner Act was a proper remedy to the situation . A superior remedy, one consistent with the free market origins of the country, would have been to repeal the NIRA. But that was politically impossible at the time.

3. *Criminal Conspiracy*

As the story goes, in the nineteenth century courts acted purposively to suppress unions by treating them as criminal conspiracies and, therefore, illegal associations. In fact, the intention of the courts was not to suppress unions as voluntary organizations pursuing collective aims in the labor market, as long as what the unions did was legal. The courts were opposed to illegal acts of unions, not to unions *per se*.

The only unions that existed in the United States in the early nineteenth century were really craft guilds of skilled workmen. In an 1806 case which many unionists like to cite to show the villainy of the courts, a group of journeymen cordwainers (shoemakers) in Philadelphia who were employed by master cordwainers formed a union and attempted to force their employers to fire all journeymen who did not belong to the union. They also attempted to prevent non-members from entering the trade. The grand jury returned an indictment which charged "that association members conspired to raise wages, refused to work for an employer who paid less than a fixed rate and prevented workers who were not members of the association from being hired."[8] The judge, stressing that the union was attempting to restrict the lawful acts of non-members, found the Philadelphia Cordwainers guilty and fined them.

In 1809 in New York and in 1815 in Pittsburgh there were similar cases involving cordwainers, and the judgments of the courts were the same. It simply is contrary to the principles of voluntary exchange that a group would attempt to restrict the price offers made by others and prevent those others from obtaining employment from willing employers.

In 1835, in *People v. Fisher*, a New York court rendered a definitive verdict in a case involving another union of shoemakers:

> The man who owns an article of trade or commerce is not obliged to sell it for any particular price, nor is the mechanic obliged to labor for any particular price. He may say that he will not make coarse boots for less than one dollar per pair, *but he has no right to say that no other mechanic shall make them for*

less. The cloth merchant may say that he will not sell his goods for less than so much per yard, *but he has no right to say that any other merchant shall not sell for a lesser price*. If one individual does not possess such a right over the conduct of another, no number of individuals can possess such a right. All combinations therefore to effect such an object are injurious, not only to the individual particularly oppressed, but to the public at large....[9]

It is clear that the court, far from trying to suppress the legitimate right of people to organize for common ends, was merely reminding the parties of the rules of voluntary exchange—the rules of natural law. An individual can make whatever price offer he wants, but he cannot restrict the price offers of others. Since groups get their rights from the rights of individuals that make them up, what an individual cannot do a group cannot do.

In 1842, in *Commonwealth v. Hunt*, the Massachusetts Supreme Court rendered a verdict that unionists claim marked the end of the illicit use of the criminal conspiracy doctrine against unions. According to one college text in labor law:

The landmark American decision...covering the basic legality of labor combination, when utilized for proper purposes, is *Commonwealth v. Hunt* .... Since the rendition of this decision the right of American labor to organize has not been seriously questioned by either the courts or legislatures.[10]

In fact, as the cordwainer cases and especially *People v. Fisher*, made clear, the right of American labor to organize was already firmly established. The First Amendment to the United States Constitution guarantees the freedom of association to all people. The issue is: Do the organizations undertake actions which trespass on the natural rights of others—especially workers who do not want to be labor union members? The prosecuting attorney in *Commonwealth v. Hunt* charged:

The defendants formed a society the object of which was...What? That they should not be obliged to work for wages which they did not think a reasonable compensation? No: If that were the sole object of the society, I approve it.... No man is to work without a reasonable compensation; they may legally and properly associate for that purpose....[11]

What the prosecuting attorney objected to was the use of compulsion of non-members as a means of achieving the desired higher wages. Although Chief Justice Shaw's opinion went against the prosecutor, it was not because the Court acquiesced in actions that denied rights to others. It was merely because the facts of the case did not demonstrate that the union had undertaken any unlawful acts. Chief Justice Shaw wrote:

Supposing the object of the association to be laudable and lawful, or at least not unlawful, are these means criminal? The case supposes that these persons are not bound by contract, but free to work for whom they please, or not to work, if they so prefer. In this state of things, we can not perceive that it is criminal for men to agree together to exercise their own acknowledged rights, in such a manner as best to subserve their own interests....

We think, therefore, that associations may be entered into, the object of which is to adopt measures that may have a tendency to impoverish another, that is to diminish his gains and profits, and yet so far from being criminal or unlawful, the object may be highly meritorious and public spirited. The legality of such an association will therefore depend upon the means to be used for its accomplishment. [12]

This ruling is perfectly consistent with *People v. Fisher*. Its one apparent innovation is the statement that some actions which may tend to reduce someone else's income may be lawful. But that is not a departure from the general principles of voluntary exchange. If I steal from person A, that is illegal. If I offer a better voluntary exchange offer to person C than person A does, and if person C accepts my offer over person A's offer, then person A's "gains and profits" are diminished. In both cases A has been "impoverished," but only the theft is illegal or immoral. What counts, to repeat Justice Shaw, is "the means to be used."

4. *Injunctions*

Unionists claim that prior to the Wagner Act courts improperly suppressed unions by issuing injunctions which forced workers, on pain of fine, imprisonment, or both, to cease lawful picketing, demonstrating, and striking. The union view of the Pullman strike of 1894 was outlined in the previous section. Members of the American Railway Union refused to handle trains that included Pullman cars. The strike was directly against the Pullman Company, but the means employed involved railroad companies other than Pullman. The union actually boycotted railroad companies that included Pullman cars in their trains. When the union members refused to do their work for those railroads, the railroad managers hired other workers who were perfectly willing to do so. The union responded violently, attempting to prevent those workers who wanted to work from doing what they were hired to do. The injunction that was obtained ordered the union to stop interfering with the replacement workers and the general operation of the railroads. Remember again, the railroads were not the direct object of the strike. The Pullman Company was. According to one witness, when the injunction was served:

The men (union members)...gathered around and I suppose there were 500 men upon the hill, in the roadway and around the cars.... It was from the

crowd that the cry came, "To hell with the Government!" "To hell with the President!" "To hell with the court and injunctions."[13]
President Cleveland supported the injunction because the mails were interfered with, and he was concerned with defending the rights of the willing workers and the railroads who were the innocent victims of the union boycott.

If workers agree to work for a specific period of time at a particular wage, they are bound to live up to the agreement for that specific period of time. I cannot justly agree to play the piano for ten nights at $200 per night starting next Saturday and then refuse to play the piano for that price next Monday. A contract, freely entered into, is legally and morally binding on all parties thereto. In the absence of such a contract an individual worker, or any group of workers, clearly has a legal and moral right to refuse to work if the wage offered is insufficient. However, there is no natural right (even though there may be a legal right) to prevent someone else who is willing to do the job from doing so. Under the Wagner Act as amended today, union members have a legal right to refuse to do a job and at the same time to prevent other willing people from taking their places. But back in 1894 no such spurious legal right existed. President Cleveland and the court were perfectly correct in trying to protect the replacement workers. Even today they would be morally correct to do so.

When the Sherman Antitrust Act of 1890 was making its way through Congress there was an unsuccessful attempt to exempt labor unions. Although labor unions are not explicitly mentioned in the Sherman Act, the language of the bill was changed to forbid trusts and "other" associations in restraint of trade.[14] It was reasonable for President Cleveland to think that the Sherman Act as well as the interstate character of the railroads empowered him to act in the Pullman strike. When the union refused to obey the injunction, the President sent in troops to enforce it.

Unionists did not like the use of injunctions under the Sherman Act. Injunctions usually called for an immediate cessation of strike activity. Once a strike is interrupted it is hard for labor union leaders to get the rank-and-file to keep up their enthusiasm. Picketing, demonstrations, and rallies can get spirits high; but once lowered those spirits are very difficult to raise again. In any case, in 1914 the Clayton Act was passed. Section 6 of the Clayton Act explicitly exempts labor unions from antitrust laws. It asserts:

That the labor of a human being is not a commodity or article of commerce. Nothing contained in the anti-trust laws shall be construed to forbid the existence and operation of labor, agricultural, or horticultural organizations instituted for the purposes of mutual help...or to forbid or restrain individual members of such organizations from lawfully carrying out the legitimate objects thereof; nor shall such organizations, or the members, thereof, be held or construed to be illegal combinations or conspiracies in restraint of trade, under the anti-trust laws.[15]

Samuel Gompers asserted that Section 6 was "Labor's Magna Charta." The formation of labor unions was now clearly beyond the reach of the antitrust laws.

But the concern of the government and the courts never had been with the formation of voluntary organizations of workers. Their concern was always with the illegal actions that were quite often carried out by such organizations. The courts continued to prosecute labor unions after 1914 whenever they engaged in illegal, coercive acts. Section 20 of the Clayton Act says:

That no restraining order or injunction shall be granted by any court of the United States...in any case between employers and employees...unless necessary to prevent irreparable injury to property, or to a property right, of the party making the application....[16]

The Clayton Act had no effect on the courts' use of restraining orders and injunctions in labor disputes precisely because the courts had never used such devices for any purposes other than those explicitly authorized by Section 20.

It was the 1932 Norris-LaGuardia Act that exempted labor unions from all aspects of antitrust and equity law, even in cases involving overt violence. As the folklore of the unionists has it, the federal government and its courts as well as state courts used the injunction vigorously throughout the first three decades of the twentieth century to quash the legitimate activities of labor union members. The shibboleth "no government by injunction" became a favorite chant at union rallies and demonstrations. The advent of the Great Depression created a lot of political and popular support for labor unions that they otherwise would not have enjoyed. That support, together with skillful lobbying by union leaders and influential sympathizers, mainly academics, led to the adoption of the Norris-LaGuardia Act.

The belief that governments had abused the injunction in dealing with labor unions prior to 1932 is pure myth. In fact, it is probably much more than that. Since the record is so accessible, it may well be that the often repeated tale is actually a purposive deception. Sylvester Petro, a Professor of Law at Wake Forest University, examined all 524 reported federal and state injunction cases during the period 1880-1932.[17] No injunctions were ever issued restricting any strike for higher wages and better working conditions. Neither was picketing enjoined unless it involved violence. As in the case of the Pullman strike, injunctions were issued against the perpetrators of violence and aggression against the rights and property of other people. It is simply amazing how any serious person can claim that unions were systematically abused before the enlightened 1930s. Less than one percent of strikes that took place between 1881 and 1932 involved federal injunctions. Less than two percent involved state injunctions.[18] And all of the injunctions involved explicit, illegal, most often violent, activities. The bald truth is that the Norris-LaGuardia Act gave unions a license to engage in violent and coercive acts as long as the acts were related to a labor dispute.

5. Yellow Dog Contracts

Section 3 of the Norris-LaGuardia Act made yellow dog contracts unenforceable in federal courts. Yellow dog contracts, as we mentioned earlier, are agreements between an employer and a potential employee that if hired the employee would not join, support, organize, or in any way affiliate with a labor union. It is unfortunate that the unionists' pejorative label for such contracts has become the standard name for them. The very name suggests that an employee who enters into such an agreement is a cowardly dog licking the boots of the master employer.

Such contracts were consistently upheld by the United States Supreme Court until the passage of the Norris-LaGuardia Act. And why not? In Chapter 1 we saw that the most basic entitlement that a person has is to his own human capital and the labor that he performs using that human capital. Each person, therefore, has a natural right to make whatever voluntary exchange offer he wants in the sale of his labor services. The buyer doesn't have to accept the offer. If a worker wants to offer a prospective employer the promise that he will not affiliate with a labor union if hired, he should be permitted to do so. If a worker can offer to refrain from smoking on the job as an inducement to the employer, why can he not offer to refrain from union activities? Moreover, if the employer, as part of his voluntary exchange offer, wants to include a requirement that a prospective employee not participate in unionism, why is that any different from requiring as a condition of employment that the employee show up for work each day at 8:00 a.m.? The employee doesn't have to accept the offered terms. Under natural law, freedom of contract is just as important as freedom of association. Indeed, without the former the latter is meaningless. Both freedoms are based upon individual self-ownership.

Now, this argument cuts both ways. A closed shop is an arrangement whereby an employer contracts with a union that he will hire only members of that union as employees. If the contract was the outcome of voluntary exchange there is nothing impermissible about it according to natural law theory. No one would say that natural law is violated if I agree with the owner of a gardening firm that I will have all of my gardening done by his employees. There is no difference between that agreement and one wherein I, as an employer, agree to buy labor services exclusively from a particular union. I hasten to add, however, that this argument does not apply to closed shops or union shops set up under the original Wagner Act or its Taft-Hartley amendments. I will have more to say about this in the next chapter. Here, the point is that the Wagner Act's closed and union shops contracts are not true voluntary exchange arrangements. Employers are coerced into recognizing a union as the exclusive bargaining agent of all employees in the first place. An employer who also agrees only to employ union members wouldn't have done so if he didn't have to submit to dealing with an exclusive bargaining agent.

Adair v. United States [208 U.S. 161 (1908)] was a famous case involving the yellow dog contract. Adair was an agent for an interstate railroad who fired an employee, Coppage, for union activities after Coppage had agreed that he would abstain from such activities. The Supreme Court declared that Adair had a right to do so under the due process clause of the Fifth Amendment:

> ...it was the defendant Adair's right—and that right inhered in his personal liberty, and was also a right of property—to serve his employer as best he could so long as he did nothing that was reasonably forbidden by law as injurious to the public interest. It was the right of the defendant to prescribe the terms upon which the services of Coppage would be accepted, and it was the right of Coppage to become or not, as he chose, an employee of the railroad company upon the terms offered to him....

> ...it is not within the functions of government...to compel any person in the course of his business and against his will, to accept or retain the personal sevices of another, or to compel any person, against his will, to perform personal services for another....[19]

The knee-jerk reaction of unionists was that this was merely another example of the Court supporting employers against workers. Lessons were learned which turned out to be very useful twenty seven years later in the writing of the Wagner Act.

But the most infamous yellow dog case in union folklore is *Hitchman Coal and Coke Co. v. Mitchell* [245 U.S. 229 (1917)]. The Hitchman Company operated a coal mine in West Virginia which employed members of the United Mine Workers of America. In 1906 the union called a strike. After two months a self-appointed committee of employees approached management with a proposal to reopen the mine on a non-union basis. The workers agreed to leave the union and, so long as they were employed by Hitchman, not to join again. The mine reopened, and all new employees were required to assent to the same nonunion pledge. After some time of successful operation on a nonunion basis, Hitchman was faced with an attempt by the United Mine Workers of America to reintroduce the union. Hitchman resisted the attempt by relying on its nonunion agreements with its employees. In January 1908 Hitchman sued the union to attempt to rid itself of harrassment. One of the arguments offered by the union was that Hitchman's employees were improperly prevented from unionizing by the so-called yellow dog contracts. The Court found:

> That the plaintiff was acting within its lawful rights in employing its men only upon terms of continuing nonmembership in the United Mine Workers of America.... Plaintiff's repeated costly experience of strikes and other interferences while attempting to "run union" were a sufficient explanation of its resolve to run "nonunion," if any were needed. But neither explanation or justification is needed. Whatever may be the advantages of "collective bargaining" it is not bargaining at all, in any just sense, unless it is voluntary on both sides.... This court repeatedly has held that the employer is as free to make nonmembership in a union a condition of employment, as the working man is free to join the union, and that this is part of the constitutional rights of personal liberty and private property, not to be taken away even by legislation unless through some proper exercise of the paramount police power....[20]

Once again the Supreme Court was steadfast in its defense of natural rights. There was no denial of workers' legitimate rights to organize involved in this case. The Court defended the legitimate right of the workers to abstain from organizing if they chose. In this case the most important fact about labor unions came into bold relief: Labor unions are organized against nonmembers who want to remain nonmembers.

Yellow dog contracts were desired by nonunion workers as protection against unions. Employers did not need them, for employment was under the common law doctrine of "at will." Employers and employees alike could terminate the employment relationship at any time unless they had made a voluntary contract to the contrary. The yellow dog contracts provided nonunion workers with some protection against union conflict because the workers could counter the efforts of union organizers with the statement that they were under contractual obligation not to join. According to Morgan Reynolds:

> Employees at Hitchman agreed to refrain from joining the union in exchange for assurance that the company would refuse to deal with the national union, hoping to avoid the disruptive union tactics which had already cost the employees so dearly in sacrificed wages. The employees accepted nonunion pledges, as did new hires, in order to resume their production and earnings.[21]

Labor unions are cartels of workers who want to quash all outside competitive sellers of labor services. The fact that they have sustained the belief among well-intentioned people that they serve all workers in the struggle against employers is testimony to the power of myth over fact.

6. *The Cause of the Great Depression*

Perhaps no belief has done more mischief than the belief that the Great Depression of the 1930s was a failure of the free market system. Ever since the 1930s governments everywhere have enthusiastically accepted the job of making the economy run right. The dominant view of the Roosevelt Administration was that low and falling prices caused the depression, and the obvious cure was to eliminate the competition that lowered prices. The National Industrial Recovery Act (NIRA) allowed employers to cartelize in order to fix and raise the prices of the goods and services produced in their firms; and it also, in Section 7(a), allowed sellers of labor services to cartelize to fix and raise the wages paid to workers. In 1935, after the NIRA was declared unconstitutional, the Wagner Act became law. It even more firmly than Section 7(a) empowered labor unions to be effective labor cartels. Such outright suppression of competition in the name of the public interest could not have occurred had it not been for the widespread belief that depressions are caused by low and falling prices and wages.

In fact, however, it is clear that the federal government itself caused the Great Depression. Moreover, the federal government has been responsible for all of the post-World War II recessions and inflations in the United States. Throughout the 1920s the federal government substantially inflated the money supply. When new money is injected into the economy it causes relative prices to change. The prices of those things the people who first get hold of the money buy rise relative to the prices of other things. Producers are misguided by those relative price changes into thinking that the real, underlying pattern of demand has changed. They respond to the relative price changes by gearing up to produce more of those things whose prices have risen. But, eventually, as the new money continues to circulate, it becomes more evenly spread out, and relative prices return to their undistorted pattern. This means that production cutbacks and layoffs will emerge as resources are redirected. The production cutbacks and layoffs are called recessions. They are merely corrections of the misdirections of resources caused by the earlier inflation of the money supply.[22] The corrections began in late 1928 and early 1929. They would have been carried out without a disaster like the Great Depression had it not been for the Federal Reserve System's monumental blunder of cutting the money supply by one third between 1929 and 1933.[23] That massive deflation of the money supply meant that on average individual money prices and wages would have to fall substantially before full employment could be restored. The cartelization of output and labor markets during the Roosevelt administration actually prolonged the Great Depression, making it worse than it otherwise would have been.

Far from ameliorating recessions and depressions, Wagner Act style unions make it much more difficult for prices in input and output markets to adjust to the distortions created by government manipulation of the money supply. The Great Depression makes an excellent case in favor of abolishing Wagner Act type labor unions.

Labor Union Legislation up to the Wagner Act

In 1926 the Railway Labor Act became law. It affected only workers on interstate railroads, and it provided that if a majority of workers voted to be represented by a particular labor union that union became the exclusive bargaining agent for all the workers. Workers who wanted to be represented by some other union as well as workers who did not want to be represented by any union were coerced into accepting the representation services of the union chosen by a majority of workers. Railroads were forced to bargain with the exclusive bargaining agent. The Act was promoted by already-unionized railroads who wanted to impose compulsory collective bargaining on their nonunion competitors. In 1934 the Railway Labor Act was amended to allow those workers who did not want to join a union or pay fees to the union to avoid doing so. The workers still had to accept the representation services of the union whether they wanted them or not, but they were protected against having to pay for the "privilege." The Act was again amended in 1951 to remove the protection against com-

pulsory membership or compulsory payment of service fees that was
granted by the 1934 amendment.

Section 7(a) of the 1933 NIRA was the first union-related federal legislation (other than the Norris-LaGuardia Act discussed earlier) that affected most labor markets. It read:

> Every code of fair competition, agreement, and license approved, prescribed,
> or issued under this title shall contain the following conditions: (1) That em-
> ployees shall have the right to organize and bargain collectively through rep-
> resentatives of their own choosing, and shall be free from the interference, re-
> straint, or coercion of employers of labor, or their agents, in the designation
> of such representatives or in self organization or in other concerted activities
> for the purpose of collective bargaining or other mutual aid or protection; (2)
> that no employee and no one seeking employment shall be required as a con-
> dition of employment to join any company union or to refrain from joining,
> organizing, or assisting a labor organization of his own choosing ; and (3)
> that employers shall comply with the maximum hours of labor, minimum
> rates of pay, and other conditions of employment, approved or prescribed by
> the President.[24]

The codes of fair competition alluded to in 7(a) were the cartel agreements reached among firms concerning their output markets. If firms were
going to cartelize their output markets they would, in exchange for that
privilege, have to recognize and bargain with labor unions chosen by their
workers. Forced bargaining was the *quid pro quo* employers had to accept
for the immunity to antitrust prosecution granted them by the NIRA.

The second condition specified that no worker could be forced to join a
company-sponsored union or to refrain from joining any labor union of his
choosing. It did not outlaw company-sponsored unions, it merely stated
that no worker could be forced to join one. A worker who freely chose to
join a company-sponsored union was free to do so. Moreover, a company-
sponsored union made up of voluntary members was a union that met the
requirements of the first condition.

The Railway Labor Act provided that a union that is chosen by a majority of workers becomes the exclusive bargaining agent for all workers.
Section 7(a) had no such provision. Under Section 7(a) there could be
proportional union representation of workers. That is, the workers at a
particular firm might choose to affiliate with different unions. Each union
would represent only those workers who chose to affiliate with it. Any
worker that did not want to be represented by any union at all would not
be. Thus, for example, at some plant 52% of the workers could be represented by Union A, 28% represented by Union B (which could be a com-

pany-sponsored union), with the remaining 20% representing themselves as individuals.

In response to Section 7(a) many employers immediately began to set up company-sponsored unions. The independent unions fought hard to try to have the government declare that company-sponsored unions were not true labor unions, but they failed. The independent unions also failed in their endeavor to have the government declare that Section 7(a) called for exclusive, rather than proportional, union representation.

Two federal agencies had the responsibility of enforcing Section 7(a) — the National Labor Board (NLB) and the National Recovery Administration (NRA). The latter agency was responsible for administering all of the NIRA, and the NLB was specifically set up to deal with labor union questions. The NLB tended to favor the positions advocated by the independent unions, while the NRA consistently supported the legitimacy of voluntary company-sponsored unions and the principle of proportional representation.[25] The dispute between the two agencies was effectively resolved on March 25, 1934 when President Roosevelt announced the settlement he had worked out between the automobile manufacturers and the unions representing the automobile workers. This famous settlement explicitly recognized the legitimacy of freely-chosen, company-sponsored unions and endorsed the principle of proportional representation.

On March 1, 1934 Senator Robert Wagner (D, NY) had introduced a Labor Disputes Bill that would have done away with company unions and proportional representation. In addition, it would have authorized exclusive bargaining agents to compel workers to either join or support the union. Immediately after the President announced his automobile settlement Senator Wagner softened his bill by removing the prohibition of company-sponsored unions and permitting previously negotiated contracts to remain in force. Yet the remaining coercive features of the bill, especially the provisions for exclusive representation and forced union support, were too strong for the Congress to swallow. The Labor Disputes Bill died in Congress.[26]

In the face of an imminent strike in the steel industry President Roosevelt dictated Public Resolution Number 44 which he sent to Congress for its endorsement. This resolution set up the first National Labor Relations Board in place of the NRA and gave the Board authority to conduct elections among workers to determine, on the basis of proportional representation, which unions would represent which workers at which plants. Public Resolution 44 became law on June 16, 1934. It did not supercede Section 7(a), it merely set up some machinery and rules for the implementation of Section 7(a) which remained in effect until May 27, 1935 when the Supreme Court declared the entire NIRA to be an unconstitutional delegation of legislative power, and also unconstitutional on the ground that it regulated *intra*state, rather than *inter*state, commerce, a power denied by the Constitution to the federal government (*Schechter Poultry Corporation v. United States*, 295 U.S. 495). After this defeat President Roosevelt jumped on the bandwagon, supporting a new bill that Senator Wagner had introduced in Congress. This new bill became the National Labor Relations Act (the Wagner Act) on July 5, 1935. As amended in 1947 and again in 1959 it still is in force. We will consider the National Labor Relations Act and its amendments in some detail in the next chapter.

The Recognition Strikes of 1933-1935

In unionist folklore there is no better period of time with which to illustrate the predatory behavior of employers against employees than 1933-1935. Even with government, through Section 7(a), finally enlisted on the side of the angels, employers allegedly continued to deny fundamental human rights to employers. Union after union tried to gain recognition of workers' rights to have unions represent them, while employer after employer, through company-sponsored unions and other devious means, resisted the workers' attempts. It took the Wagner Act of 1935 to force employers to recognize and honor workers' rights.

In reality, there is no better period than 1933-1935 to illustrate the coercive nature of Wagner Act type unions. There were hundreds of recognition strikes during those years, but they were not strikes by employees against recalcitrant employers. They were attempts by outsiders, usually assisted by a minority of employees, to force employers, against the will of a majority of their workers, to recognize the unions as the exclusive representatives of all workers in collective bargaining.

The company unions of the time were freely chosen by a majority of employees who recognized the complementarity of labor and management. Indeed, these company unions were early forms of what today is so admired in Japanese labor relations. Workers and management came together in workers councils to discuss problems and work them out. Workers and managers sought, through formal representation structures within firms, to cooperate in the promotion of the economic success of their enterprises. The outside unions emphasized struggle; the company unions emphasized cooperation.

One famous case that pitted a company's workers and their freely-chosen company-sponsored union against an outside independent union in a Section 7(a) dispute involved the Wierton Steel Co. of Pittsburgh, Pennsylvania. The case never made it all the way to the Supreme Court because it became moot when the NIRA was declared unconstitutional. However, the case was tried at the Federal District Court level, and Judge John P. Nields had it right in his decision:

> It is said that this relation (between management and workers) involves the problem of an economic balance of the power of labor against the power of capital. The theory of a balance of power is based upon the assumption of an inevitable and necessary diversity of interest. This is the traditional old-world theory. It is not the 20th century American theory of that relation as dependent upon mutual interest, understanding, and goodwill. The modern theory is embodied in the Wierton plan of employee organization.[27]

In the Fall of 1934 there was a national strike in the textile industry. The union's tactic was to send "flying squadrons" of men into plants to force the employees off the job. Sometimes the power was shut off to prevent any work from being done. Often rocks were thrown and people were beaten. Folklore tells us that the violence was employer-initiated, but in fact the aggressor was the union.[28] The union was successful in tying up "the whole industry by intimidation."[29]

On July 17, 1934 the Kohler Company of Kohler, Wisconsin was struck by 500 of its 1500 workers over the issue of union recognition. Labor relations at Kohler prior to the strike were often described as "the symbol of happy employer-employee relations."[30] The clear majority of workers was content with the company-sponsored union that had worked out the harmonious labor relations within the firm, but the employees decided to hold an election to determine how much support the outside union had. When a huge majority voted to be represented by the company-sponsored union, the outside union refused to recognize the election results.[31]

Time and time again the same story was reenacted. In the Spring of 1935 the Sawmill and Timber Workers Union tried to force workers to accept their representation services. An industry-sponsored union, the Loyal Legion of Loggers and Lumbermen, was chosen by most workers as their Section 7(a) representative. The outside union attempted to shut down operations in Pacific Northwest mills. In Bridal Veil, Oregon, 125 employees of one mill voted 110 to 15 to continue to support the Loyal Legion. In response the outside union sent in 400 pickets from Portland to shut the plant down. In Tacoma, Washington, workers formed a committee of employees to ring the doorbells of all employees to get them to sign a petition against the outside union in order to reopen the struck mills. Sixty-eight percent of those on the payroll before the strike signed the petitions. The Governor of Washington then sent in troops to protect employees against violence from the outside union.[32]

In April 1935 an outside union of rubber workers boasted that only "one-sixth union membership is sufficient to close down a plant through mass picketing."[33] There were about 35,000 workers employed by the Goodyear, Firestone, and Goodrich companies in Akron, Ohio at the time. The outside union claimed 12,000 of those workers as members. Nevertheless, a strike was called, plants were shut down, and incomes were lost—all in the name of what? All in the name of forcing workers to affiliate with a union, a union not freely chosen by most of them. Yet, this is another chapter in what is conventionally thought of as labor's long and bitter struggle for social justice.

The record is clear: The unions' long and bitter struggle was not against employers, it was against workers who understood the complementarity between labor and management and wanted to remain free from the forced cartelizaton of labor. John L. Lewis, the leader of the United Mine Workers Union and the first president of the Congress of Industrial Organizations, candidly summed up the purpose behind his sort of union when in 1901, at a meeting of Midwest miners, he said:

> As I understand it, it is for the purpose of wiping out competition, between us miners first, viewing it from our side of the question; next for the purpose of wiping out competition as between the operators in these four states. When we have succeeded in that and we have perfected an organization on both sides of the question, then as I understand the real purpose of this movement, it is that we will jointly declare war upon every man outside of this competitive field....[34]

These words confirm the basic thesis of this chapter: that traditional unions are organized against all individuals who are not members of the union.

NOTES

1. Lewis Paul Todd and Merle Curti, *Rise of the American Nation* (New York: Harcourt Brace Jovanovich, 1977) p. 449.

2. W. H. Hutt, *The Strike-Threat System*, (New Rochelle, New York: Arlington House, 1973) p. 23.

3. F. A. Hayek (ed.), *Capitalism and the Historians* (Chicago: University of Chicago Press, 1954).

4. *Ibid.*, p. 12.

5. Irving Bernstein, *The New Deal Collective Bargaining Policy* , (Berkeley: University of California Press, 1950) pp. 5-6.

6. *Ibid.*, p. 90.

7. *Ibid.*, p. 146.

8. Clarence B. Carson, *Organized Against Whom?*, (Alexandria, Virginia: Western Goals, 1983) p. 22.

9. *Ibid.*, p. 22. Emphasis added.

10. A. Howard Myers and David P. Twomey, *Labor Law and Legislation*, (Cincinnati: South-Western Publishing Co., 1974) pp. 7-8.

11. Carson, *op. cit.*, p. 22.

12. Myers and Twomey, *op. cit.*, pp. 9-10.

13. Carson, *op. cit.*, p. 42.

14. *Ibid.*, p. 43.

15. Henry Steele Commager, *Documents of American History*, Volume II, Sixth Edition, (New York: Appleton-Century-Crofts, 1958) p. 280.

16. *Ibid.*, p. 281.

17. Sylvester Petro, "Injunctions and Labor Disputes: 1800-1932," *Wake Forest Law Review*, June 1978, pp. 341-576.

18. Morgan O. Reynolds, "An Economic Analysis of the Norris-LaGuardia Act, the Wagner Act, and the Labor Representation Industry," *Journal of Libertarian Studies*, forthcoming, MS. p. 17.

19. Commager, *op. cit.*, p. 226.

20. Myers and Twomey, *op. cit.*, pp. 15-16.

21. Reynolds, *op. cit.*, p. 9.

22. Murray Rothbard, *America's Great Depression*, (Kansas City: Sheed and Ward, 1972).

23. Milton Friedman and Anna Schwartz, *A Monetary History of the United States, 1867-1960*, National Bureau of Economic Research, (Princeton: Princeton University Press, 1963).

24. Bernstein, *op. cit.*, p. 37.

25. James A. Gross, *The Making of the National Labor Relations Board*, Volume I (1933-1937), (Albany: State University of New York Press, 1974) pp. 10-15.

26. *Ibid.*, pp. 68-69.

27. *Business Week*, March 2, 1935, p. 14.

28. *Business Week*, September 15, 1934, pp. 20-21.

29. *Ibid.*, p. 36.

30. *Business Week*, August 18, 1934, pp. 12-16.

31. *Business Week*, October 20, 1934, p. 1.

32. *Business Week*, June 29, 1935, p. 16.

33. *Business Week*, April 13, 1935, p. 7.

34. Carson, *op. cit.*, p. 10.

Chapter 3

Current Labor Union Law: A Critique

> In no country do the decisions of positive law coin-
> cide exactly, in every case, with the rules which the
> natural sense of justice would dictate. Systems of
> positive law, therefore, though they deserve the
> greatest authority, as the records of the sentiments of
> mankind in different ages and nations, yet can never
> be regarded as accurate systems of the rules of natural
> justice.
>
> Adam Smith
> *The Theory of Moral Sentiments*
> 1759

The Wagner Act, officially called the National Labor Relations Act
(NLRA), was adopted in 1935. It was amended in 1947 and renamed the
Labor Management Relations Act (LMRA) or the Taft-Hartley Act. The
LMRA was amended again in 1959 by what is called the Landrum-Griffen
Act. The official name of the federal law that governs unionism in the pri-
vate sector in the United States today is the Labor Management Relations
Act; however, it is quite common for people to refer to today's law as the
National Labor Relations Act as amended . The term I use in the remainder
of this monograph is simply the National Labor Relations Act (NLRA).
When I want to discuss the original 1935 Act itself, I call it the Wagner
Act. My critique is focused on the Wagner Act and its 1947 Taft-Hartley
amendments. The 1959 Landrum-Griffin Act was directed specifically at
the problems of corruption and crime in labor unions. It was designed to
give the rank-and-file union member some protection against the predatory behavior of union officers. Although those issues are, of course, important, my chief concerns are with the coercive features of unionism
which are not only legal, but are promoted by government in the Wagner
Act and the Taft-Hartley Amendments.

Exclusive Representation

Section 9(a) of the NLRA states:

Representatives designated or selected for the purposes of collective bargaining by the majority of the employees in a unit appropriate for such purposes, shall be the exclusive representatives of all the employees in such unit for the purposes of collective bargaining in respect to rates of pay, wages, hours of employment or other conditions of employment....[1]

Section 9(c) specifies the procedures that must be followed in determining which union, if any, is to act as an exclusive bargaining agent. When "a substantial number of employees" want to be represented by a union and the employer does not grant exclusive bargaining status to the union, a secret ballot election is held under the auspices of the National Labor Relations Board (NLRB), the administrative and quasi-judicial agency set up specifically to carry out the provisions of the NLRA. Each union that can demonstrate that it has "substantial" support among the employees must appear on the ballot, and a "no representative" option must also appear on the ballot. The winner of the election is that ballot choice that receives fifty percent plus one or more of the votes cast. If there is no winner on the first round, there must be a secret ballot runoff between the two choices that got the most votes.

The NLRA does not define what constitutes a "substantial" number of employees for the purposes of Section 9(c). In practice the NLRB considers a 30% showing of support to be substantial. When a union is seeking exclusive bargaining agent status it tries to get employees in the bargaining unit to sign "authorization cards" which are simply declarations that the employees who sign want the union to be their bargaining agent. When a union receives a sufficient number of signed authorization cards it goes to the employer and asks for recognition as the exclusive bargaining agent. If the employer does not agree to extend this recognition, the union calls on the NLRB to hold the secret ballot representation election.

The NLRB decides which employees are in which bargaining unit. Sometimes all the employees at a plant are put into one bargaining unit, and sometimes several bargaining units are designated by the NLRB within one plant. This gives the NLRB significant influence over the outcome of representation elections. For example, it can split up the anti-union vote into minority groups within different bargaining units so that an exclusive bargaining agent is imposed on all employees.

A union that is seeking exclusive bargaining agent status approaches employees face-to-face when it asks them to sign authorization cards. There is, therefore, a large potential for intimidation. Individual employees may sign only because they are afraid not to sign. Moreover, once an employee signs an authorization card the NLRB refuses to hear any testimony or consider any complaints that the signatures were collected under duress. A signed card, no matter how the signature was obtained, is as good as gold to the union.[2]

It is important to note that a union that acquires exclusive bargaining agent status represents all employees in the bargaining unit. It represents those employees who want the winning union to represent them, but it also represents those employees who want to be represented by some other union as well as those employees who do not want to be represented by any union. Each employee in the bargaining unit who does not want the representation services of the winning union loses the right to select his own agent in the sale of his own labor services. He cannot even represent himself. The basic axiom of natural rights theory, the axiom of self ownership, is thrown out the window. Dissident employees no longer fully own their own labor. Full ownership implies that a worker individually can choose his own agent or even individually choose to use no agent in the sale of his labor services.

President Roosevelt's 1934 automobile settlement (see Chapter 2) honored the axiom of self-ownership, but the NLRA does not. The automobile settlement, you will recall, was based on proportional representation with the right of self-representation preserved for those who chose it. Under the proportional representation, union A represents only those workers who freely choose to be represented by union A. The automobile settlement was based on voluntarism; the NLRA is based on coercion.

Those who defend the principle of exclusive representation in unionism do so on the basis of an analogy with congressional, or other governmental, elections. For example, Irving Berstein makes the argument this way:

> Majority rule, of course, entails a loss of some minority rights. Groups that favor a minority union or minorities that prefer no union are saddled with the majority bargaining agent. By the same token, citizens who vote for an unsuccessful Democratic candidate for Congress must accept representation by a victorious Republican. This is the expedient cost of a workable democratic system....
>
> Behind [the Wagner Act] lay a groundwork of political theory stemming from the eighteenth century Enlightenment, democratic standards against which to measure new conditions. In essence these ideas stated that citizens were entitled to representatives of their own choosing, that democratic secret ballot

elections under universal suffrage with majority rule were the best means of selection....[3]

But this analogy is totally inappropriate. *Unions are not governments.* In Chapter 1 we saw that according to the political theory of the Founding Fathers, a legitimate government arises out of a social contract among the governed which grants government a monopoly on the legal use of force, explicitly for the limited purpose of enforcing the proscription of involuntary exchange. Since, by definition, a government has a monopoly on the legal use of force there can be only one government in a political jurisdiction. All people must accept the protective and judicial services of the monopoly government. The election of representatives to wield the coercive powers of government must be on the basis of exclusive representation because there is no other way for the governed to control what the monopoly government does. Democratic theory of the Enlightenment was a theory of government, and only government. It was never a theory of the operation of private associations or clubs. Enlightenment theory made a clear separation between the governmental sphere and the private sphere. Mandatory submission to the will of a majority was reserved for the governmental sphere. The operating principle in the private sphere was *individual* freedom of choice.

Labor unions are private associations of private people. As such they have no right, under natural law, to coerce any nonmember to go along with what a majority of members and supporters want to do. Government has a monopoly on the legal use of coercion. Coercion by unions, even under the cloak of majority rule, is still coercion. It is a clear violation of natural law. As a unanimous Supreme Court said in *Carter v. Carter Coal Co.* [298 U. S. 238 (1936)] when it threw out the Bituminous Coal Conservation Act (the Guffey Coal Act) which included exclusive bargaining agent unionism as one of its features:

> The effect, in respect of wages and hours is to subject the dissenting minority, either of producers or miners or both, to the will of the stated majority.... To accept, in these circumstances is not to exercise a choice, but to surrender to force.

> The power conferred upon the majority is, in effect, the power to regulate the affairs of an unwilling minority. This is legislative delegation in its most obnoxious form; for it is not even delegation to an official or an official body, presumptively disinterested, but to private persons whose interests may be and often are adverse to the interests of others.... And a statute which attempts to confer such power undertakes an intolerable and unconstitutional interference with personal liberty and private property.[4]

The NLRA blurs the distinction between the governmental sphere and the private sphere. It moves toward a politicization of private decision-making. Those who today are attempting to promote "economic democracy" by advocating laws that give workers a legal right to determine the operations of private enterprises through majority voting are merely pushing the NLRA to its logical conclusion. Economic democracy is not a new idea at all. It is a very old and dangerous idea. It is a prescription for the demise of individual liberty.

Senator Robert Wagner (D, NY) consistently advocated compulsory unionism throughout the 1930s. He was chairman of the National Labor Board under Section 7(a) of the National Industrial Recovery Act, and he was author of both the original Labor Disputes Bill (1934) and the Wagner Act. He summed up his philosophy of economic democracy this way:

> The development of a partnership between industry and labor in the solution of national problems is the indispensable complement to political democracy. And that leads us to this all-important truth: there can no more be democratic self-government in industry without workers participating therein, than there could be democratic government in politics without workers having the right to vote.... That is why the right to bargain collectively is at the bottom of social justice for the worker, as well as the sensible conduct of business affairs. The denial or observance of this right means the difference between despotism and democracy.[5]

Apparently, Senator Wagner had an agenda much broader than securing the worker's right to organize. He was interested in securing worker participation in all sorts of industry decision-making. His vision was of a corporate state wherein government, industry, and unions form a troika to work out all of the affairs of government and private life.

Compulsory Bargaining

Section 8(a)5 of the NLRA declares that it is an unfair labor practice for an employer

> to refuse to bargain collectively with the representatives of his employees subject to the provisions of Section 9(a).

This is a verbatim adoption of Section 8(5) of the Wagner Act. The NLRA, however, goes on to say in Section 8(d) that

> For the purposes of this section to bargain collectively is the performance of the mutual obligation of the employer and the representative of the employees to meet at reasonable times and confer in good faith...but such obligation does not compel either party to agree to a proposal or require the making of a concession....

An employer is compelled to bargain "in good faith" with a union that gains exclusive bargaining agent status. This, too, is a violation of natural rights. The natural right to participate in voluntary exchange with others does not imply that you can bargain with whomever you wish. It means that you may bargain with any *willing* other party you wish. That this is so is obvious when we recognize that it is logically impossible for everyone simultaneously to have the right to bargain with whomever he or she wishes. If I have a right to bargain with B in the sense that B must bargain with me whether he wants to or not, then B does not have the right to bargain with whom he wishes. He does not wish to bargain with me, and when he is coerced to do so, his alleged right to choose his bargaining mate is denied. We do not have a right to choose a bargaining mate. We do have a right only to choose a *willing* bargaining mate. Voluntary exchange is based on *mutual* consent.

If American unionism was based on the voluntaristic ethic of Samuel Gompers, there would be no legal duty to bargain imposed on anyone. Unions would represent only those workers who freely associated with them, and employers would be free to decide whether or not to bargain with the unions. An employer would decide whether or not to bargain with union A based upon the alternatives he or she faced at the time. If there were sufficient other unions that were offering to bargain with the employer, or if there were sufficient individual workers seeking to bargain, the employer could well decide not to consent to union A's offer to bargain. It would, to a great degree, depend on union A's reputation and record for reasonable bargaining and execution of contracts. Unions would be competing with unions and self-represented workers.

There is no argument, of which I am aware, that can justify compulsory bargaining on grounds consistent with natural law. Those who defend compulsory bargaining must logically reject the natural law constraint. Irving Bernstein, again, provides a good example of such an argument:

> By definition collective bargaining, like any contractual relationship, entails a mutuality of obligation for agreement to be reached. To argue that the employer (or the union) may at will refrain from bargaining is to negate the process, to argue by analogy for a marital system in which only women and not men proceed to the altar. If the policy of the United States, as both the Wagner and Taft-Hartley Acts declare, is to encourage "the practice and procedure of collective bargaining," the conclusion is inescapable that employers and unions alike must bargain in good faith. The NLRA, in fact, would have been an empty shell in the absence of this assumption. Why prevent employers from interfering with the self-organization of their employees if they need not

engage in bargaining?[6]

But in the absence of a voluntary exchange contract there is no "contractual relationship" between any two parties. Any contractual relationship is defined by the agreement. Prior to the agreement there is no contractual relationship. The NLRA forces a relationship to exist between an employer and an exclusive bargaining agent, but it cannot be called a "contractual" relationship. Moreover, the analogy misses the mark. In America at least the marital system is based on the idea that both parties have freely consented to enter into the marriage before anyone proceeds to the altar. The statement that without compulsory bargaining the NLRA would be an "empty shell" is not a logical defense of compulsory bargaining. It doesn't address itself to the essential nature of compulsory bargaining and how that nature squares with prior constraints. It is merely an assertion of the result of the absense of compulsory bargaining. Perhaps most people would be better off if the NLRA were an empty shell.

The "good faith" requirement of Section 8(d) of the NLRA adds even more compulsion to compulsory bargaining. The law does not define what that term means, but its meaning has become clear through the history of NLRB cases wherein some operational meaning to "good faith" had to be determined. One authority has summed up the NLRB's interpretation of good faith this way:

> Employers must do more than just meet with the representatives and merely go through the motions of bargaining. To satisfy the requirement of collective bargaining, an employer must bargain in "good faith." In defining the term, the Board held that an employer to bargain in good faith "must work toward a solution, satisfactory to both sides, of the various proposals and other affirmative conduct." In another case, the Board declared that "...the obligation of the Act is to produce more than an empty series of discussions, bargaining must mean more than mere negotiations...." The Board has considered counter-proposals so important an element of collective bargaining that it has found the failure to offer counter-proposals to be persuasive of the fact that the employer has not bargained in good faith.[7]

In practice, then, even though Section 8(d) asserts the contrary, to bargain in "good faith" means that the employer must make concessions during the bargaining. Reasonable counter-proposals are simply compromises with the union's demands.

The meaning of good faith bargaining is very important. For example, although an employer is legally entitled to hire replacement workers during any strike, when the strike is over the strikers are legally entitled to get the jobs back. They must be reinstated immediately in the case of an unfair labor practice strike, and they must be reinstated as soon as their replacements leave in the case of an economic strike. An economic strike is one over wages, hours, and other conditions and terms of employment. In practice, therefore, when a strike is called over economic issues the employer is often compelled immediately to reinstate the strikers because should he fail to do so the union would simply assert that the failure to reach agreement over the economic issues was a result of the employer's failure to bargain in good faith which is an unfair labor practice. The NLRB's record demonstrates that it is usually sympathetic to such allegations.

The Right to Strike

Section 13 of the NLRA explicitly guarantees the right of all employees to participate in primary strikes. A primary strike is one of a union of employees of an employer against that employer. Secondary strikes are not permitted. That is, a union cannot strike or picket an employer other than the one by which its members are employed. Such secondary strikes and picketing were outlawed by the 1947 Taft-Hartley amendments to the Wagner Act.

When unionists talk about the right to strike they mean the right of a union of employees to refuse to work, to set up picket lines, to prevent people from crossing those picket lines, and to maintain their status as employees during and after the strike. When the strike is settled those on strike have a right to go back to work, displacing any workers that were hired during the strike. Such a set of rights, it is alleged, is implicit in the freedom of association guaranteed by the First Amendment. However, not all parts of that set of rights are consistent with natural law. Certainly, in the absence of a current contract to the contrary, any individual worker or group of workers has the right to refuse to work if the terms of trade offered by the employer are unsatisfactory. That right is a direct implication of the axiom of self-ownership. But when an individual worker or a group of workers does so, it does not have any right to maintain the status of employee. If the terms of trade are turned down, the worker or group of workers is free to make a counter-offer or to seek employment elsewhere. The worker or group of workers has no just property rights to jobs it refuses to do. Section 2(3) of the NLRA says that the term "employee" includes "any individual whose work has ceased as a consequence of, or in connection with, any current labor dispute...," but that is a legislated privilege, not a natural right.

While picketing on public rights-of-way is within the constraints of natural law, prevention of people from crossing picket lines is an explicit act of violence against others, and is not within those constraints. Group A can refuse to engage in voluntary exchange with person B, but person B can, then, simply seek out some willing group C with which to transact. Any interference by group A with person B or group C constitutes trespass against their natural rights. If group A is a local lodge of the Masons, person B is the owner of a regalia shop, and group C is the local lodge of the Sons of Norway, no one would object to the previous two sentences. But as soon as group A is a labor union, person B is an employer, and group C is an association of independent workers, many people do object. I maintain there is no substantive difference in the principles involved in both cases. The fact that many people, perhaps most people, are willing to grant special privileges and apply special rules when unions are involved is further testimony to the power of myth over fact and sentimentality over reason.

Union Security

Section 8(3) of the Wagner Act says that it is an unfair labor practice for an employer

> By discrimination in regard to hire or tenure of employment...to encourage or discourage membership in any labor organization *Provided*, that nothing in this Act...shall preclude an employer from making an agreement with a labor organization...to require as a condition of employment membership therein, if such labor organization is the representative of employees as provided in section 9(a)....

Section 8(a)3 of the NLRA inserts, after "membership therein," the words "on or after the thirtieth day following the beginning of such employment or the effective date of such agreement, whichever is the later." Finally, Section 14(b) of the NLRA says:

> Nothing in this Act shall be construed as authorizing the execution of application or agreements requiring membership in a labor organization as a condition of employement in any State or Territory in which such execution or application is prohibited by State or Territorial law.

While both the Wagner Act and the NLRA force employers throughout the country to recognize and bargain in good faith with a union that acquires exclusive bargaining agent status under Section 9(a), both laws only *permit* exclusive bargaining agents and employers, as part of collective bargaining contracts, to agree to force all workers to acquire membership in the exclusive bargaining agent as a condition of employment. The Wagner Act permitted a "closed shop" wherein workers had to be union members before they could even begin employment, but the NLRA permits only a "union shop" wherein workers must join the union after they are employed for thirty days.

Moreover, Section 14(b) of the NLRA lets individual states and territories outlaw even the union shop or other forms of union security agreements. As of this writing twenty states—the *"right to work" states*—have outlawed the union shop. Some of these states have gone further and outlawed the "agency shop" and "maintenance of membership" forms of union security as well. The *agency shop* is an agreement between an exclusive bargaining agent and an employer that requires those workers who choose not to join the union, to pay "service fees" to the exclusive bargaining agent. Under a *maintenance of membership agreement* any worker that is a member of the union that has exclusive bargaining agent status when a collective bargaining contract is signed must continue to be a member of that union until the collective bargaining contract expires.

All of the various types of "union security" agreements—closed shop, union shop, agency shop, and maintenance of membership—are designed to protect the exclusive bargaining agent from workers who do not want to support the union. Unionists claim that such agreements are legitimate because the law forces an exclusive bargaining agent to represent *all* employees in a bargaining unit whether the employees want to be so represented or not. Since the union must represent everyone it is only just, the unionists argue, that everyone contributes to the support of the union. If individual workers could choose not to support the exclusive bargaining agent, they would get the representation services, and the alleged benefits thereof, for free. Such workers would be "free riders," or "free loaders." Since Section 14(b) was added to the NLRA in 1947 unionists have used the free rider argument to try to get Congress to repeal Section 14(b). The same argument is used by unionists in individual states to try to defeat the adoption of "right to work" laws in the thirty states that do not have them and to try to repeal "right to work" laws in the twenty states that do have them.

But the "free rider" argument is without merit. First of all, it was the unions themselves that fought a long and bitter battle against the principle of proportional representation with individual workers having the right to choose to remain independent. The American Federation of Labor under

William Green fought against President Roosevelt's automobile settlement and supported Senator Wagner's original Labor Disputes Bill as well as the 1935 Act on the grounds that exclusive representation was the only acceptable arrangement. It isn't as if federal law importuned the unions to accept the burden of exclusive representation. Exclusive representation is itself an unjust privilege that federal law granted to unions at the unions' behest. For the unions then to go on and say that the burden of exclusive representation justifies union security arrangements is at best disingenuous. If unions want to be free of the burden of free riders, all they have to do is to lobby the Congress in favor of the repeal of Section 9(a) of the NLRA. Instead, they heap one injustice on top of another and advocate the repeal of Section 14(b). Section 14(b) would be meaningless without Section 9(a). As long as the principle of exclusive representation is in force workers need protection against further coercion by unions. Section 14(b) gives them that protection in the twenty "right to work" states. In my judgment, unless we can abolish the principle of exclusive representation, the protections afforded by Section 14(b) ought to be extended to workers in all states.

There are other reasons why the unions' "free rider" argument does not justify the subjection of workers to union security arrangements. In the next chapter we will see that there is an abundance of empirical evidence that suggests that unions do not generate very many benefits for workers. In brief, there is precious little benefit that any independent workers gets from the representation services of exclusive bargaining agents. There is nothing on which the free rider can ride. Moreover, even if unions could demonstrate that they generate pecuniary gains for all those they represent, there is still the problem of subjective costs. A worker who gains some money income from a union's representation services could still be a net loser from those services if he or she disliked affiliating with the union so much that the subjective losses offset the pecuniary gains. There is simply no way that such subjective costs can be measured. There is no way that a union could prove that a free rider is getting something for nothing. If the independent worker was forced to support the union he could well be a *forced rider*.

When union security arrangements are in effect there is at least one set of definite free riders—the union officers. When workers are coerced into joining a union or supporting a union as a condition of employment union officers don't have to worry very much about doing a good job for the workers. In an open shop, where workers decide for themselves whether to join or support the exclusive bargaining agent, the union officers constantly have to strive to make workers believe they are doing a good job. Workers will not support union officers who don't perform unless they are forced to do so. The fact that union officers can be voted out of office by the rank-and-file doesn't exert as much discipline on union officers as an open shop does. In an open shop workers don't need to wait until election time or attend union meetings to exert their influence. They can simply stop contributing money any time they choose. Similarly, although Section 9(c)(1)(A)(ii) of the NLRA provides for decertification elections, workers still don't have as much protection against union officers as they do in an open shop. At least 30% of the eligible workers must petition for such a decertification election before the NLRB will begin to set one up. Moreover, no such election may be held within one year of any valid representation election, and the NLRB will not entertain a petition for decertification except during a thirty day period within sixty to ninety days before the expiration of an existing collective bargaining contract.

Finally, in order to emphasize the relevant issues, it is useful to reconsider the relationship between closed shop (or any union security) agreements and yellow dog contracts. In voluntary exchange contract theory each party can make whatever offer he wants to anyone who freely chooses to consider such an offer. The only constraint is that the voluntary exchange rights of third parties cannot be impaired thereby. Thus, an employer has a right, as part of his job offer, to specify that if the potential worker accepts the employment he will totally abstain from all union activity. If the potential employee doesn't like that feature of the job offer he can make a counteroffer or simply look for employment elsewhere. If the employee accepts the job offer he is justly bound by its terms for the period of time specified in the hiring agreement. Yellow dog contracts are clearly permissible in voluntary exchange contract theory (i.e., contract theory based on natural law). Similarly an employer is within his voluntary exchange rights to make mandatory union membership a part of his job offer. If a potential employee finds the offer unacceptable, he can make a counteroffer or seek employment elsewhere. If the employee accepts the job offer, he is bound by its terms for the period of time specified in the hiring agreement. Closed shop (or any union security) agreements *per se* are, also, clearly permissible in voluntary exchange contract theory. This is the reason that Milton Friedman said that he is opposed to "right to work" laws.[8]

However, "right to work" laws have been passed within the context of mandatory recognition of exclusive bargaining agents. Employers who have negotiated union security agreements with exclusive bargaining agents with which they are forced to bargain have not done so within a context of voluntary exchange. They have not freely chosen to bargain with the union in the first place, much less to bargain on the specific issue of union security. In my judgment, right to work laws are justifiable counter-measures to the coercion implicit in compulsory bargaining with exclusive bargaining agents. If we didn't have compulsory bargaining with exclusive bargaining agents, right to work laws couldn't be justified. But neither would they be needed.

Freedom of Speech and Association

It is common for unionists to appeal for support by asserting that labor unions are justified by workers' freedom of association. Similarly, picketing and union political activity are justified by the same workers' freedom of speech. I have already pointed out that freedom of association implies the freedom of individuals to choose those with whom they will associate, and that the principle of exclusive representation is a flagrant denial of that right. But there is another dimension to the issues of the freedom of association and speech. Unions are politically very active. Dues money is used by unions to support some political candidates and oppose others. Dues money is also used to lobby in favor of some policies (involving such non-labor issues as environmentalism and abortion) and in opposition to others. Dues money collected from workers who freely choose to be union members could reasonably be considered voluntary contributions, and there isn't any reason in natural law to limit what a union can do with such money as long as the rank-and-file are kept fully informed of the decisions being made by the union officers. However, many union members are members against their will. If they had their choice they would not be members, and they would not pay any dues. Similarly, many workers are compelled to pay service fees to unions that represent them against their will. If these workers had their way they would not pay such fees. When union officers use money collected from people who are compelled, against their will, to make such payments to support political candidates and political and social activities of which the workers do not approve, there is a clear violation of both freedom of association and speech.

Fortunately, the courts have recognized the constitutional issues involved in the spending of coerced payments collected from unwilling workers. In 1977, in *Abood v. Detroit Board of Education*, the Supreme Court declared that agency shop contracts in the public sector are constitutional, but the Court also declared that the service fees collected from nonmembers can only be used to pay direct collective bargaining and grievance administration costs.[9] All money collected from nonmembers that was used for impermissible purposes had to be refunded. Unfortunately, the Court did not specify the procedures to be used in determining how much of a refund is due in those cases involving money already collected, nor did it spell out an acceptable procedure to use to limit the future collection of fees from nonmembers to those amounts to be used for permissible purposes. The details of such procedures will, it seems, be spelled out in future cases.

Two such cases are of particular interest. In May 1983 the Supreme Court agreed to hear arguments in *Ellis/Fails v. Brotherhood of Railway, Airline and Steamship Clerks*. In this case two hundred California airline employees alleged that the union used their compulsory union dues for partisan political and idelogical activities of which they did not approve. The union had set up a rebate scheme, but union functionaries sat as both judge and jury within the scheme, and the workers alleged they were not granted the full refund they deserved. A Federal District Court in San Diego ruled in 1980 that such spending violated the rights of the workers and ordered refunds, but in September 1982 the Ninth Circuit U.S. Court of Appeals reversed the lower court.[10] It is widely expected that the Supreme Court will use *Ellis/Fails* to build on the *Abood* precedent and more completely spell out workers' rights.

The *Abood* case involved workers' rights under a state statute involving public sector workers. The *Ellis/Fails* case involves workers in the private sector under the Railway Labor Act. A third case, *Beck v. Communications Workers of America*, involves workers' rights under the NLRA. In March 1983 a U.S. District Court judge in Baltimore ruled that 79% of the dues collected from eighteen workers had been spent for impermissible purposes and must be refunded.[11] The union has appealed this decision, and it is widely expected that this case will eventually be decided by the U.S. Supreme Court.

As of this writing, it seems clear that every worker who is forced to turn over money to a union as a condition of maintaining employment can force the union to open up its books and account for how it spends its revenue. Needless to say, unions are not delighted with this state of affairs. They could avoid it all simply by not collecting money from unwilling workers, but they probably will try to change the law in the direction of reducing the rights of workers to have any say over how union service fee and dues income is spent. Whenever unions are given a choice between more coercion and less coercion they always seem to pick the former.

Senator Jesse Helms (R, NC) and Congressman William Dickinson (R, AL) have introduced federal legislation that would specifically outlaw the use of money forcefully collected from workers for any partisan political or ideological purposes. At this writing there does not seem to be enough support in the Congress to pass the legislation. The issue, it seems, will have to be decided by the courts on the basis of current labor law.

The Constitutionality of the Wagner Act

We have seen many reasons in this chapter why the Wagner Act could reasonably be called unconstitutional. Indeed, based on the Supreme Court's decision in the 1935 *Schechter* case (the case that threw out the National Industrial Recovery Act) and its decision in the 1936 *Carter* case (the case that threw out the Guffey Coal Act) most observers at the time expected the Supreme Court to throw out the Wagner Act. In a strong attack on the Wagner Act, a *Business Week* editorial writer put it this way:

Business will not obey the edict. It will not submit to a onesided Act of Congress that forbids employers to interfere with regular labor unions but does not forbid the American Federation of Labor to interfere with company unions. It is manifestly the intention of Congress to unionize American business. Unjust as this compulsion is, business would yield to it if it were lawful. But it is not. It is injustice aggravated by usurpation. It is a piece of despotism which business will unitedly resist. It will be fought to the finish; and unless all the signs are deceptive, it will finish on its back.[12]

President Roosevelt had trouble finding eligible people to serve on the NLRB right after the law was passed in 1935 because, as Gross puts it, the *Schechter* case "left little doubt in most minds that the Wagner Act would not survive the inevitable Supreme Court case."[13]

Even some Wagner Act proponents in the Congress expressed doubt that the Act could pass constitutional muster. Congressman C. V. Truax (D, OH) let everyone know that he wasn't going to let the Constitution stand in the way of his voting in favor of the Act. He exclaimed:

We see the same old faces that oppose all progressive humanitarian legislation.... What are you going to do with the sacred old Constitution? You cannot eat it, you cannot wear it, and you cannot sleep in it.[14]

A better example of the end-justifies-the-means rule of political decision making could not be found.

One of the arguments the Court had used to throw out the National Industrial Recovery Act in the *Schechter* case was that the Constitution permits the federal government to regulate only interstate commerce; and production within a state, even if the product later moves in interstate commerce, is not interstate commerce. This principle, that production is not commerce, was also used by the Court in the *Carter* case to throw out the Guffey Coal Act. After the *Carter* case in 1936 the members of the NLRB became frustrated and dejected. They sent a "highly confidential" memorandum to all regional boards telling them that because of the *Carter* decision it didn't appear that any union cases involving manufacturing rather than direct interstate commerce had much chance of being successfully pursued.[15]

On April 12, 1937 the Supreme Court announced its pro Wagner Act decision in *NLRB v. Jones & Laughlin Steel Corporation* [301 U.S. 1 (1937)]. By a 5-4 vote the Court upheld the constitutionality of the Wagner Act. Before the decision President Roosevelt had grown weary of the Court throwing out so much of his New Deal legislation. The *Schechter* decision particularly infuriated him. The President reminded the nation that the Constitution does not specify how many judges must sit on the Supreme Court. On February 5, 1937, four days before the Supreme Court heard oral arguments on the Wagner Act, he announced that he planned to expand the Court, packing it with judges who would see things his way. The *Jones & Laughlin* decision has always been called the "switch in time that saved nine." At least five votes were needed to sustain the Wagner Act, and the Court had in the previous term unanimously thrown out the Guffey Coal Act. Because of the intense political pressure five Supreme Court votes were mustered to approve the Wagner Act. In exchange, the President dropped his Court packing plan.

The Supreme Court, like all branches and agencies of government, follows the election returns. President Roosevelt had been reelected by a landslide in November 1936. He clearly had the political clout that would be needed to pack the Court. A prudent majority of the Court simply reinterpreted a few pahses of the Constitution, and the threat went away. The Constitution says what the Supreme Court chooses to say it says. The interpretive choices made by the Court depend on the political views of its members and their reading of the political realities of the moment as well as their legal reasoning. Supreme Court justices are, after all, mere mortals, albeit with incredible power.

But the change in the thinking of the Court between *Schechter* and *Jones & Laughlin* may not be that surprising after all. In *West Coast Hotel v. Parrish* [300 U.S. 379 (1937)], announced one month before *Jones & Laughlin*, the Supreme Court finally removed the people's constitutional protection of substantive due process in all economic matters. Both the Fifth and the Fourteenth Amendments say that government may not deprive citizens of life, liberty or property without due process of law. When interpreted substantively that means that the government cannot interfere with the freedoms of citizens unless there is some overriding, compelling reason for it to do so. When it does so the burden of proof is on the government to demonstrate that there is sufficient reason for what it does. Prior to *West Coast Hotel v. Parrish*, in a whole string of cases, especially *Lochner v. New York* [198 U.S. 45 (1905)] and *Adkins v. Children's Hospital* [261 U.S. 525 (1923)], the Supreme Court had applied the strictures of substantive due process to economic regulation as well as attempted regulation of such things as speech and the press. In *Lochner* the issue was an attempt by the state of New York to set maximum working hours in bakeries. In *Adkins* the issue was minimum wage legislation. The Court threw out both attempts to regulate economic exchange on the grounds that such regulation violated the strictures of substantive due process.

In his dissent in the *Lochner* case Justice Oliver Wendall Holmes made a distinction between people's economic rights and their other liberties. He implied that economic rights do not merit the protection of substantive due process. He claimed that the majority decision was based "upon an economic theory which a large part of the country does not entertain." He demonstrated what a vulgar majoritarian he really was by stating that a majority had a right to "embody their opinions in law" no matter how "tyrannical" or "injudicious" the resulting regulations may be. He went on to state that "the libery of a citizen to do as he likes so long as he does not interfere with the liberty of others to do the same" is nothing but a "shibboleth."[16] As Thomas Haggard puts it, Holmes dismissed as a shibboleth "what has long been the cornerstone of most natural—and individual-rights theories."[17] Holmes simply replaced the doctrine of the divine right of kings with the equally oppressive doctrine of the divine right of majorities. Fortunately, at that time, Holmes was in the minority.

But in *West Coast Hotel v. Parrish*, Holmes' view became the majority view, and substantive due process was cast aside in favor of procedural due process in matters of economic regulation. Life and (noneconomic) liberty were still protected by substantive due process, but property was, now, to be protected only by procedural due process. Under procedural due process the government can pass and enforce any regulation it wants as long as it follows the correct legislative and administrative procedures in doing so. The government is assumed to have the right to impose economic regulation under the police powers of the state, and the burden of proof rests on those who would argue differently. The police powers of the government are its powers to protect the health, safety, morals, and general welfare of the public. All a government has to do to meet the requirements of procedural due process is to assert that the economic regulation under question is an exercise of its police powers.

The shibboleth that supporters of the Holmesian view use to gain support for their position is that "human rights come before property rights." Now there is a truly empty slogan. There cannot be any legitimate distinction between property rights and human rights because property rights *are* human rights. They are the rights of humans to use that which they own for their own purposes subject only to the constraint that they cannot engage anyone else in involuntary exchange while doing so. When the specious reasoning of Oliver Wendall Holmes became the majority view of the Court it was almost certain that room would be found in the Constitution for the coercion of the Wagner Act.

Public Sector Unionism

In January 1962 President John F. Kennedy issued Executive Order 10988 authorizing collective bargaining on the Wagner Act model for federal employees. Wages and salaries were outside the scope of federal collective bargaining, and strikes by federal workers continued to be illegal; but exclusive representation and compulsory bargaining were imposed on federal workers and government agencies at the behest of union leaders who had supported the President in the 1960 election campaign. That Executive Order was soon followed by legislation in state after state authorizing compulsory collective bargaining on the Wagner Act model for state and local employees. Most of this state legislation permits bargaining over wages and salaries and some even permits strikes by public employees.

Compulsory unionism for federal workers was continued by Executive Orders from Presidents Johnson, Nixon, Ford, and Carter. It was made permanent by the Civil Service Reform Act of 1978. Table 3-1 shows the dramatic increase in the unionization of government employees at both the federal and state and local level during the 1970s. In 1980 nearly 50% of all government employees were unionized.[18] This is all the more remarkable when it is realized that less that 20% of the civilian labor force is unionized.

Table 3-1

Public Sector Unionization-Percent of Employees Unionized

Year	All Government	Federal	State and Local
1970	32.5%	51.7%	27.2%
1972	33.9	51.9	29.3
1974	37.7	52.6	34.2
1976	39.1	48.8	37.0
1978	39.8	59.3	35.5

Source: Myron Lieberman, *Public-Sector Bargaining*, (Lexington, MA: Lexington Books, 1980), p. 4.

Whatever one thinks of the appropriateness of Wagner Act type unionism in the private sector, and my chief objection thereto is its coercive nature, such arrangements are clearly inappropriate in the public sector.

1. *Public Sector Unionism Diminishes Democracy*

Matters that come under the scope of collective bargaining (e.g., wages and salaries, fringe benefits, working hours, work loads, work procedures, and working conditions) are, in the public sector, matters of public policy. The U. S. Constitution and the constitutions of the individual states provide that public policy—i.e., the actions of government as it spends taxpayers' money—can only be determined by the legislative branch of government with the concurrence of the executive. All branches of government are subject to carefully prescribed procedures wherein citizen taxpayers have access to government in the deliberations that lead up to the adoption of public laws and budgets. All taxpayer citizens are supposed to have open access to government in its deliberations. No private citizen or private group of citizens is supposed to have special access to govenment as it sets public policy. Moreover, no legislature or executive can delegate its constitutional powers to any private individual or group.

But collective bargaining on the Wagner Act model means that a private club (an association of private citizens who happen to be government employees) does get special access to government in the determination of public policy. Matters that come under the scope of collective bargaining are determined in closed door collective bargaining sessions between private clubs and appointed or elected officials of government. Agreements are reached which involve the spending of taxpayer money, and those agreements, and their concomitant taxes, are then imposed on taxpayers. The whole system amounts to nothing other than taxation without representation.

An egregious example of this taxation without representation recently took place in Rhode Island. A school board had negotiated a pay raise with a teachers' union. The school district ran out of money and ceased paying the wage increase. The union sued, and the Rhode Island Supreme Court upheld the union, stating that "the lack of funds affords no legal basis for disavowal of...the agreement." The Court instructed the school district to make provisions "for the imposition and collection of a tax which will be used to pay the outstanding judgment."[19] In July 1983 the San Jose School District in California declared bankruptcy because a California court forced the District to honor wage increases granted in an earlier collective bargaining agreement. It remains to be seen whether a tax will be imposed on all District, or even State, taxpayers to honor the collective bargaining agreement.

Unionists assert that democracy is not diminished by public sector bargaining because taxpayer voters can always vote scoundrels who enter into unacceptable collective bargaining agreements out of office. But taxpayer voters are subjected to the tax burden of such agreements as soon as they are made. Voting the scoundrels out in two or four years does not protect taxpayer wallets against agreements when they are reached.

Unionists go on to argue that the threat of being tossed out of office will assure that government officials will not enter into collective bargaining agreements that are displeasing to voters. But this argument is especially naive. Politicians know that individual voters make their voting decisions on the basis of one or two issues that are particularly important to them at election time. Voters are typically willing to overlook a lot of what are to them minor transgressions of a politician if the politician votes in favor of the government program that focuses its benefits on them. Almost every government program has sharply focused benefits. Each program, in other words, benefits a relatively small number of particular people in significant ways. But the costs of each program are spread out over *all* taxpayers. Each voter, as beneficiary of a particular program, has a direct and intense incentive to lobby in its favor; but as a taxpayer that same voter has no countervailing incentive of equal intensity to lobby against any program. His or her share of the costs of any particular program, no matter who is benefitted therefrom, is too small to call forth a countervailing lobbying campaign. This is why government expenditures at all levels inexorably grow. Moreover, unions are highly organized associations. Union support at election time is extremely valuable. Union people can operate phone banks, run carpools, put up posters, and otherwise support favorite candidates. Most government officials will be willing to impose a tax burden that is spread out over all taxpayers in exchange for the support of a grateful labor union.

In order to avoid public sector strikes, especially by police and firefighters, some government jurisdictions use compulsory arbitration to settle their collective bargaining disputes over wages and salaries and other terms of employment. A presumably neutral third party is brought in to determine what the public employees' wages and salaries will be. But this is an even more obvious imposition of taxation without representation. The arbitrator gets to decide what taxes taxpayers will have to pay to meet the terms the arbitrator imposes. There is little or no difference between King George's tax on tea and King Arbitrator's wage tax.

2. *Exclusive Representation in the Public Sector*

To my knowledge all laws that explicitly authorize public sector collective bargaining provide for exclusive representation. Representation elections are held among the public employees in a bargaining unit, and the union that gets 50% plus one or more of the votes cast is the exclusive bargaining agent for all employees in the unit. Only the union that gains exclusvie bargaining agent status can represent those employees to the government or government agency that employs them. This places a private club between taxpayer citizens who are employed by government and the government that employs them. Abraham Lincoln once reminded us that in the United States government is supposed to be of, by, and for all the people. No private agency is supposed to be able to intervene between citizens and their government. If a citizen wants to address his or her government on matters of public policy, no private agency is supposed to block his direct access to that government. If a citizen wants to request that his government improve a public street, no private agency is supposed to intervene. If a citizen who also is a public employee wants to request that his government improve his wage or working conditions, no private agency is supposed to intervene. Most people would be outraged if all requests for public street improvement had to be made through a cartel of private local construction companies. To be logically consistent, they should also be outraged when all requests by citizens who are public employees for wage improvements must be made through a private cartel imposed on those public employees.

I have no quarrel with those public employees who freely choose to be represented by a union in the sale of their labor services. What I object to is a system under which every public employee, whether he wants to or not, must go through a union that has exclusive bargaining agent status in order to deal with his own government.

3. *Compulsory Bargaining in the Public Sector*

In the United States democratically elected government is supposed to wield the sovereignty of the people. The people, acting through their democratically elected government, are sovereign. To be sovereign is to have a monopoly on the legal use of force. No private agency is supposed to have any coercive power over the democratically elected government of the sovereign people. Yet under Wagner Act style bargaining in the public sector governments are forced to recognize, and bargain in good faith with, private clubs that acquire exclusive bargaining agent status. This is a clear infringement of the sovereignty of the people. Unions assert that government has chosen to set up the compulsory bargaining and, thus, has not surrendered the people's sovereignty. But government has no legitimate right to diminish the people's sovereignty in that way. Government cannot legitimately delegate its responsibility to wield the people's sovereignty.[20]

The only sort of collective bargaining that would be legitimate in the public sector would be voluntary bargaining between governments or government agencies as employers and labor unions that represent only those workers who freely choose to join them. Moreover, because tax money is involved and public policy is being determined, the bargaining sessions would have to be open to the public with provision for taxpayer-voter participation. Finally, any agreement reached would have to be subject to ratification by the legislative and executive branches of government. Better still, ratification by the people themselves through direct referendum could be required.

4. *Union Security Agreements in the Public Sector*

Not all public sector collective bargaining laws permit union security agreements; but many, especially those applying to public school teachers, do. The typical union security agreement in the public sector is the agency shop. Workers do not have to join the union that has exclusive bargaining agent status to maintain their public employment, but they have to pay service fees to the union in order to continue to be employed by the goverment or government agency for which they work. The "free rider" argument is used to justify these public sector union security agreements just as it is used to justify similar arrangements in private employment. The arguments expressed earlier in this chapter aginst union security arrangements in the private sector can be used here as well. But there is a very special question that arises when union security agreements are imposed in the public sector. Stripped down to its bare essentials, a union security arrangement in the public sector means that a taxpayer-citizen must pay tribute to a private club for the privilege of working for his own government. A private association of private people says: If you don't give us money we will have the government fire you. This is simple blackmail and extortion. When Lincoln described American government as one of the people, by the people, and for the people, he did not add: as long as they pay tribute to the Masons, or to the Knights of Columbus, or the Rotary or the National Education Association (NEA).

Teachers at all levels have historically been immune to being fired because they have, after some trial period, been granted tenure. Once granted tenure a teacher or professor cannot be fired except under very extreme conditions. Tenure has long been defended by teachers' unions on the ground that it is needed to protect academic freedom. Before it became a labor union the NEA staunchly defended tenure rights. With tenure no Senator Joseph McCarthy could have a teacher or professor fired simply for expressing views in the classroom with which Senator McCarthy disagreed. The NEA became a labor union in the 1960s. As soon as it obtained exclusive bargaining agent status it set about negotiating union security agreements. Under such agreements tenure protects teachers and professors from being fired for every reason *except* not paying tribute to the NEA. Teachers and professors usually cannot even be fired for gross

incompetence, but they can be fired if they don't pay service fees to the
NEA. If the NEA were anything other than a labor union it would be
roundly denounced as hypocritical. Since it is a labor union it is cheered
for protecting itself against free riders.

5. Strikes in the Public Sector

A strike is a collective withholding of labor services and the prevention
of others from providing substitute labor services. Government is a
monopoly supplier of protective services. Indeed, the most important
function of government is to protect people against predation—i.e.,
against involuntary exchange. According to social contract theory, that is
the only reason that government was set up in the first place. When government employees who are hired specifically to provide the protective
services of government go on strike, citizens have no substitute providers
of those services to whom to turn. Government officials must hire substitute employees to provide those services, or else there simply is no effective government at all. When strikers attempt through picketing, violence,
and intimidation to prevent substitutes being hired they are attempting by
force to shut the government down. The sovereignty of the people, wielded
through their democratically elected government, is thereby denied. The
strikers claim the right to use force to shut down that institution that is
supposed to have a monopoly on the legal use of force. The only appropriate
response is for the government to arrest and prosecute the strikers for
insurrection. But if the police are on strike, who will do the arresting? If
the police are on strike, who wields the coercive authority of government?
Does government exist in any meaningful sense at all?

Answers to those questions are suggested by the experience of San
Francisco during the 1970, 1974, 1975, and 1976 public employee
strikes.[21] The citizens of San Francisco were simply denied the basic protective services of government. For example, during the 1975 police and
fire strike, in the face of exlicit picket line violence that prevented
nonstrikers from doing their jobs, the Alioto administration refused to request help from the Highway Patrol or the National Guard. The mayor said
he didn't want to be accused of being a strike breaker. The city could burn,
the citizens could be victimized by criminals, and their health could be impaired by raw sewage being discharged into the Bay, but Mayor Alioto
wasn't going to be seen as a strike breaker. There is only one word that ac-
curately describes the San Francisco situation: anarchy. There simply

wasn't any government during those strikes. Surely, no one would argue that governmental protective services are necessary some of the time and not necessary whenever government employees that provide those services decide to go on strike. Government either is a necessary institution or it is not. If we can do without government some of the time, why can we not do without government all of the time?

The case against government employee strikes is not as strong in cases involving government services that can readily be provided by the private sector as it is in the case of governmental protective and judicial services. For example, strikes by government garbage collectors can be handled simply by contracting out the garbage collection job to private firms, and strikes by government school teachers could be handled simply by contracting out with private schools. In fact, except for the basic protective and judicial services that government was originally created to provide, the most efficient way for government to provide services to citizens is through contracting out. Strikes by government workers who provide such services may be blessings in disguise. They call attention to private sector alternatives to direct government provisions of services.

Nevertheless, all strikes against government are a challenge to the people's sovereignty that government wields. For one set of workers to refuse to do a government job and at the same time attempt to prevent others who are willing to do the job from doing so, is a direct attack against government. It does not differ in essence from insurrection and revolution. If people want to participate in a revolution against government they must recognize that if the revolution fails it is proper for government to punish them. None of the American Founding Fathers ever claimed that King George III wouldn't have the right to punish them if the British won the Revolutionary War. Certainly, none of them expected King George to sit down and do nothing for fear of being called a strike breaker.

There is another difference between strikes in the private sector and strikes in the public sector. In the private sector when a strike occurs the production of the goods and services produced by the struck firm ceases. The customers of the struck firm do not go on paying for the goods and services they no longer receive. In the case of government worker strikes, however, taxes to pay for the services continue to be assessed and collected even when the services are not provided. This is a clear case of outright theft. If General Motors could somehow force car buyers to continue to pay for new cars even though the new cars weren't being produced, those car buyers would think their basic rights were being denied. They would rightly think their money was being stolen because they received nothing in exchange for the money. When school teachers go on strike the property taxes that pay their salaries still have to be paid. Taxes are paid and no service is received in exchange. Taxpayers could rightly consider this to be another example of simple theft.

6. *In Conclusion*

George Meany, the late president of the AFL-CIO, once wrote:

The United States Congress, like any other human institution, has made its share of blunders over the years. In the field of labor-management relations, one of the most grievous was the singling out of...government workers for exclusion from the protection of the National Labor Relations Act of 1935.

By that action the Congress trampled on the principle of equal justice under law. It relegated large numbers of free and equal human beings to a category of second-class citizenship.... In recent years a great many federal, state, and local agencies have begun to contract-out to private employers work that had previously been done by government employees, work such as street, park, and building maintenance, trash collection, and similar tasks. In many cases the same workers have continued to do the same work in the same buildings, only drawing their paychecks from a different source. These workers serve the same public, but they are free to organize unions, negotiate contracts, pursue grievances, and strike, if necessary, while their fellow workers still on government payrolls are not.

Such anomalies vividly point up the arbitrariness with which public employees are discriminated against, and they further increase the resentment public employees feel.[22]

To George Meany there were no significant differences between employment by government and employment by a private firm. Apparently, he thought that government was just another economic enterprise offering goods and services to customers. Since he was blind to the essential nature of government, we should not be surprised that he thought kindly of the 1935 Wagner Act. He probably didn't understand the difference between compulsion and voluntarism.

NOTES

1. All direct quotations from the Wagner Act are taken from Irving Bernstein, *The New Deal Collective Bargaining Policy* (Berkeley: University of California Press, 1950), Appendix, pp. 153-60. All direct quotations from the NLRA are taken from A. Howard Myers

and David P. Twomey, *Labor Law and Legislation*, fifth ed. (Cincinnati: South-Western Publishing Co., 1975), Appendix, pp. 509-32.

2. John G. Kilgour, *Preventive Labor Relations* (New York: AMACOM, 1981), p. 189.

3. Bernstein, *op. cit.*, pp. 137-38, 147.

4. Edwin Vieira, Jr. "Compulsory Public Sector Collective Bargaining: The Trojan Horse of Corporativism," *Government Union Review* , Winter 1981, p. 67.

5. Bernstein, *op. cit.*, p. 28.

6. *Ibid.*, p. 138.

7. Quoted in Clarence B. Carson, *Organized Against Whom?* (Alexandria, Virginia: Western Goals, 1983), p. 55.

8. Milton Friedman, *Capitalism and Freedom* (Chicago: University of Chicago Press, 1962), p. 115-17.

9. *Abood v. Detroit Board of Education* 431 U.S. 209 (1977).

10. *Foundation News Advisory*, National Right to Work Legal Defense Foundation, December 1982.

11. *National Right to Work Newsletter*, National Right to Work Committee, March 31, 1983.

12. *Business Week*, July 6, 1935, p. 40.

13. James A. Gross, *The Making of the National Labor Relations Board*, Volume I (1933-1937) (Albany: State University of New York Press, 1974), p. 149.

14. Bernstein, *op. cit.*, p. 123.

15. Gross, *op. cit.*, pp. 198-201.

16. Henry Steel Commager, *Documents of American History*, Volume II, sixth edition (New York: Appleton-Century-Crofts, 1958), p. 221.

17. Thomas R. Haggard, "Government Regulation of the Employment Relationship," in Tibor Machan and M. Bruce Johnson, eds., *Rights and Regulation* (San Francisco: The Pacific Institute, 1983), Chapter 1.

18. Morgan Reynolds, "Cause and Effect in Public Sector Unionism: An Economic Analysis," *Government Union Review*, Winter 1983, p. 3.

19. Charles W. Baird, *Unionism and the Public Sector* (Los Angeles: International Institute for Economic Research, Original Paper 15, August 1978), p. 9.

20. See Sylvestor Petro, "Sovereignty and Compulsory Public-Sector Bargaining," *Wake Forest Law Review*, March 1974, pp. 25-165.

21. For a thorough account of this experience see Randolph H. Boehm and Dan C. Heldman, *Public Employees, Unions, and the Erosion of Civic Trust* (Frederick, MD: University Publications of America, Inc., 1982).

22. In A. Lawrence Chickering, ed., *Public Employee Unions* (San Francisco: The Institute for Contemporary Studies, 1976), pp. 165, 168-69.

Chapter 4

Effects and the Solution

> The role of the economist in discussions of public policy seems to me to be to prescribe what should be done in the light of what can be done, politics aside, and not to predict what is "politically feasible" and then to recommend it.
>
> Milton Friedman
> *Essays in Positive Economics*
> 1953

I recommend that the National Labor Relations Act as amended in 1947 and 1959, the Railway Labor Act, the Norris-LaGuardia Act, and all of the state laws that set up Wagner Act type collective bargaining for state and local employees be repealed. No laws need to be passed to take their place. All that is needed to assure justice in labor markets is a firm enforcement of the rules of voluntary exchange. The most likely first reaction to such a radical proposal is that it is politically impossible. It may be, but the only way that one can promote good public policy is to make sound arguments as often and as persuasively as possible. Public and political opinion change very slowly, but they do change when the correct arguments become widely understood.

The most likely second reaction to such a radical proposal is that workers would be impoverished if they didn't have unions to protect them. But my proposal would not destroy voluntary labor unions. It would merely remove the coercive powers that labor unions now have. Moreover, unions in fact have done very little to improve the lot of working people as a group.

Empirical Evidence on Unions' Effects on Wages and Income

Three different types of empirical studies have been done by economists on the impact of unions on wages and incomes of working people. The first type compares the wage rates paid to unionized workers to the wage rates paid to nonunionized workers, the second type compares the income shares earned by workers in unionized industries to the income shares earned by workers in nonunionized industries, and the third type compares the shares of total national income going to employee compensation, corporate profits, and proprietors' incomes. Only the results of the first type of study are consistent with the hypothesis that unions have beneficial effects for their members.

Table 4-1 summarizes the results of the most significant studies of the first type. A worker's income is the product of the wage rate he is paid and the number of hours that the worker works. Table 4-1 indicates that unionized   workers   do   receive   higher   wage   rates   on   average   than

Table 4-1: Summary of Type One Studies

Researcher and Date of Study	Percent by Which Union Wage Rate Exceeded Nonunion Wage Rate
H. G. Lewis 1963	10-15%
L. W. Weiss 1966	20%
F. P. Stafford 1968	18-52%
A. Throop 1968	25% in 1950 30% in 1960
S. Rosen 1969	38% in highly unionized industries 10% in lightly organized industries
P. Ryscavage 1974	12%

Source: Dan C. Heldman, James T. Bennett, and Manuel H. Johnson, *Deregulating Labor Relations* (Dallas: The Fisher Institute, 1981), p. 113.

nonunionized workers. This does not mean they receive higher incomes. Standard economic theory predicts a positive impact of cartelization on price. After all, if competition between sellers of automobiles were wiped out by an agreement among those sellers all to charge the same prices, prices of automobiles would probably be higher than they would be in the presence of competition. The same result is reasonably expected in the case of a cartelization of sellers of a particular type of labor service. In the absence of Wagner Act enforcement of the labor cartel, it would disintegrate and competitive wage rates would be restored. But exclusive representation, compulsory bargaining, and union security agreements all defend such labor cartels against competition.

The job of a labor union, as far as wage rates are concerned, is to restrict the supply of a given type of labor relative to the demand for it in order to increase the wage rates paid. By limiting employment to those who are admitted to union membership or pay fees to unions, unions have some power to limit supply. Before the 1947 Taft-Hartley amendments to the Wagner Act unions could use the closed shop to restrict supply. Workers couldn't even begin employment unless they first had a union card. Defacto closed shops still exist in those industries where unions operate hiring halls. One has to be a member of the union that runs the hiring hall in order to get employment. Under the union shop workers do not have to have a union card to get hired, but they have to join a union after a thirty day probationary period. Thus, a union has less control over the supply of labor than it would in a closed shop. Nevertheless, it still has more control over the labor supply than it would in an openly competitive labor market.

Although the empirical results summarized in Table 4-1 are consistent with the hypothesis that unions do, on average, raise the wage rates paid to their members relative to the wage rates paid to nonunionized workers, it is also consistent with the hypothesis that unions have simply sought to gain exclusive bargaining agent status in those industries that would have paid higher wage rates than other industries even without the union. We cannot be sure that the wage rates paid in the unionized industries are higher than they would be in *those same* industries without unionization because we cannot measure what competitive wage rates would be in those industries. It could be that these type one studies give unions credit for what would have occurred anyway even without the unions.

In any event, in order for a union successfully to raise the wage rate paid to unionized workers in any employment, it must reduce the supply of labor relative to its demand in that employment. This means that the displaced and excluded labor will have to seek employment elsewhere. Thus, the supply of labor in these other employments is increased relative to its demand, and wage rates in those employments will be lower than they otherwise would be. Union wage rate gains must come at the expense of wage rates paid to other workers.

In a very significant empirical study of the second type, Norman J. Simler examined incomes paid to workers as a percent of value added in unionized industries and nonunionized industries. He wanted to see whether increases in workers' shares of income were related in any way to the degree of unionization or changes in the degree of unionization. What he found, for the thirty-six industries for which data were available in both periods 1899-1933 and 1935-1955, was that if anything unionization was associated with lower income shares for union workers than for nonunion workers.[1]

Clark Kerr, in another type two study, found that the share of total value added that was paid to workers in unionized industries was lower than the share of total value added paid to workers in all manufacturing industries together over the period 1929-1950. His results are summarized in Table 4-2.

Table 4-2: Labor's Share of Value Added

Year	Labor's Share in Unionized Industry	Labor's Share in All Manufacturing
1929	69.1%	73.1%
1947	70.1	71.5
1950	61.7	66.1

Source: Clark Kerr, "Labor's Income Share and the Labor Movement," in George W. Taylor and Frank C. Pierson, eds., *New Concepts in Wage Determination* (New York: McGraw-Hill Book Co., 1957), p. 284.

There are no type two studies, of which I am aware, that come to different conclusions. There is no evidence, in other words, that even remotely supports the contention that labor unions help workers get their "fair share" of the incomes generated in business firms. Some union workers are paid higher wage rates than they otherwise would be, but the share of income going to workers in unionized industries is no higher, and in some cases it is even lower, than the share of income going to workers in nonunionized industries. Any unionized worker who receives an income share that is higher than it would be without the union must do so at the expense of some other worker in the same industry who ends up with an income share that is lower than it would be without the union. When a union officer claims that union security arrangements are necessary to prevent some workers from free riding on union-generated benefits, one ought to ask: What benefits?

If Wagner Act style unionism benefitted labor as a class at the expense of owners of capital, the functional distribution of national income (its division between labor and capital) should have been altered in labor's favor after the dramatic victories of compulsory unionism in 1935 and 1937. Type three studies have consistently shown that such was not the case. Any gains in income enjoyed by some workers had to come at the expense of other workers, because capital's share of national income has been unaffected by unionism.

Table 4-3 shows the percents of U.S. national income represented by compensation to employees (labor's share), and accounting profits earned in corporations and unincorporated businesses (employers' share). The first point of interest is the large jump in the employee compensation percentage and accompanying large drop in the corporate profits percentage for the period 1931-1934. These were the worst years of the Great Depression, and the resulting income shares forcefully underscore the point made in Chapter 1 that employers are residual claimants who bear most of the risk of bad times. Workers were "unprotected" by compulsory unionism during those years, but employers were not able to take advantage of that fact. The next point of interest is the fact that 1935 and 1937 do not mark the beginning of any increase of labor's share. Indeed, anyone looking at Table 4-3 without prior knowledge of the significance of those years would not pay any particular attention to them at all. Significant increases in labor's share didn't occur until the late 1960s and especially the decade of the 1970s. But those increases cannot be due to unionism. The percentage of the active labor force represented by labor unions declined in the 1960s and 1970s.[2] The reason for the increase of labor's share in this period is the explosive growth in government employment that took place then. Government employee wages and salaries are included in employee compensation figures, but there is no employers' income to go along with it. Thus, both corporate and proprietors' accounting profit must decline as a percent of national income.

Robert A. Nisbet very effectively sums up the evidence from all three types of studies of the economic effects of unions on workers.

G. K. Chesterton once wrote: 'The rational lover would never marry; the rational solider would never fight.' To which I add: the rational worker would not organize. If he were purely and exclusively rational, he would know or quickly learn how much farther he travels who travels alone. He would most certainly discover that, propaganda from union headquarters notwithstanding, the rise in wages and improvement in working conditions during the last two centuries has little to do with the activities of labor unions.[3]

Table 4-3. Percents of National Income

Year	Employee Compensation	Corporate Profits	Nonfarm Proprietors' Income
1929	60.3%	10.8%	10.4%
1930	63.4	8.0	10.0
1931	67.8	2.2	9.5
1932	73.3	−4.0	8.2
1933	73.9	−4.3	8.0
1934	70.4	2.0	9.4
1935	66.0	4.6	9.5
1936	66.7	7.6	10.3
1937	66.2	7.7	9.8
1938	68.2	5.7	10.3
1939	67.5	7.4	10.2
1940	65.4	10.9	10.5
1941	63.2	13.7	10.6
1942	62.8	14.2	10.5
1943	64.7	13.9	10.2
1944	66.6	12.9	10.2
1945	68.2	10.5	10.7
1946	66.2	9.3	12.1
1947	66.4	11.4	10.6
1948	64.6	13.2	10.6
1949	66.4	12.6	11.0
1950	65.5	14.3	10.5
1951	66.5	14.0	9.9
1952	68.5	12.4	9.8
1953	69.9	11.8	9.5
1954	69.7	11.6	9.5
1955	68.6	13.6	9.5
1956	70.2	12.4	9.3
1957	70.8	11.6	9.3
1958	70.9	10.3	9.4
1959	70.4	12.1	9.2
1960	71.6	11.3	8.6
1961	71.6	11.0	8.6
1962	71.1	12.0	8.2
1963	71.0	12.3	8.0
1964	70.9	12.9	8.1
1965	70.0	13.6	7.8
1966	70.6	13.2	7.5
1967	71.9	12.1	7.4
1968	72.8	12.0	7.2
1969	74.4	10.6	6.8
1970	76.3	8.5	6.4
1971	75.8	9.0	6.2
1972	75.1	9.7	6.1
1973	75.1	9.3	5.7
1974	77.1	7.4	5.4
1975	76.6	7.8	5.2
1976	76.3	9.3	5.2
1977	76.1	9.5	5.2
1978	75.6	9.7	5.2
1979	75.8	9.2	5.1
1980	75.2	8.6	5.0

Source: *Survey of Current Business*, U.S. Department of Commerce, October 1978, p. 55; July 1980, p. 14; July 1981, p. 12.

Most workers have nothing to lose from the abolition of compulsory unionism, but they have a lot to gain: their freedom to choose.

Compulsory Unionism and Labor Peace

A particularly persistent myth, one that has endured a clear history of empirical evidence to the contrary, is that the enactment of compulsory bargaining laws on the Wagner Act model assures peace and harmony in union-management relations. Section 1 of the original Wagner Act asserts:

> Experience has proved that protection by law of the right of employees to organize and bargain collectively safeguards commerce from injury, impairment, or interruption, and promotes the flow of commerce by removing certain recognized sources of industrial strife and unrest, by encouraging practices fundamental to the friendly adjustment of industrial disputes....[4]

That is a most extraordinary claim. Table 4-4 shows the number of strikes and their mean duration in each year during the period 1927-1980. The record speaks for itself. When compulsory bargaining was imposed on workers and employers an era of industrial strife and economic waste began. Even during World War II the number (but not the duration) of strikes was much higher than before the days of Wagner Act "peace and harmony."

The same claim of peace and harmony has been made in support of compulsory unionism legislation for state and local employees. For example, New York's Taylor Act asserts that:

> This Act (is) to promote harmonious and cooperative relationships between government and its employees and to...assur(e) the orderly and uninterrupted operations and functions of government.[5]

Certainly the people of San Francisco did not enjoy "the orderly and uninterrupted operations of government" during the 1970s. But that did not stop the California Legislature from adopting the Berman Act, the compulsory unionism law for higher education, in 1978 on the pretense of promoting peaceful labor relations on state college and university campuses.

The most intensely unionized group of public employees is public school teachers. Thirty-one states have imposed Wagner Act type compulsory bargaining laws on public school teachers. The record of labor peace in public schools is well known. At the beginning of each school year the newspapers are filled with stories of teacher strikes. Teachers

Table 4-4: Work Stoppages in the United States 1927-1980

Year	Number	Mean Duration in Days	Year	Number	Mean Duration in Days
1927	707	26.5	1957	3,673	19.2
1928	604	27.6	1958	3,694	19.7
1929	921	22.6	1959	3,708	24.6
1930	637	22.3	1960	3,333	23.4
1931	810	18.8	1961	3,367	23.7
1932	841	19.6	1962	3,614	24.6
1933	1,695	16.9	1963	3,362	23.0
1934	1,856	19.5	1964	3,655	22.9
1935	2,014	23.8	1965	3,963	25.0
1936	2,172	23.3	1966	4,405	22.2
1937	4,740	20.3	1967	4,595	22.8
1938	2,772	23.6	1968	5,045	24.5
1939	2,613	23.4	1969	5,700	22.5
1940	2,508	20.9	1970	5,716	25.0
1941	4,288	18.3	1971	5,138	27.0
1942	2,968	11.7	1972	5,010	24.0
1943	3,752	5.0	1973	5,353	24.0
1944	4,956	5.6	1974	6,074	27.1
1945	4,750	9.9	1975	5,031	26.8
1946	4,985	24.2	1976	5,648	28.0
1947	3,693	25.6	1977	5,506	29.3
1948	3,419	21.8	1978	4,230	33.2
1949	3,606	22.5	1979	4,827	32.1
1950	4,843	19.2	1980	3,885	35.4
1951	4,737	17.4			
1952	5,117	19.6			
1953	5,091	20.3			
1954	3,468	22.5			
1955	4,320	18.5			
1956	3,825	18.9			

Source: *Analysis of Work Stoppages, 1980*, Bureau of Labor Statistics Bulletin 2120, March 1982, p.8.

who want to teach and students who want to learn are intimidated by threats and acts of violence. School children are provided with excellent role models each fall. Children are taught to break the law and even participate in or threaten violence in order to get what they want. And all of this is made possible by compulsory bargaining laws that promise labor peace. Table 4-5 sets the record straight. On average states with compulsory bargaining laws have almost twice as many public school teacher strikes as those without such laws. When account is taken of the different number of school districts in each state, it is seen that states with compulsory bargaining laws have over five times the number of public school teacher strikes as states without such laws.

Table 4-5: Teacher Union Bargaining and Strikes
(January 1972 - December 1982)

States	Average Number of Teacher Strikes per State	Average Number of Teacher Strikes per 100 School Districts per State
Nationwide per state average	30.8	13.1
31 states with compulsory bargaining laws	37.9	18.9
19 states with no compulsory bargaining laws	19.3	3.7

Source: *Government Union Critique*, Public Services Research Foundation, February 11, 1983, p. 4.

Another effect of compulsory collective bargaining for public school teachers is suggested by Figure 4-1. There are two teachers' unions in the United States—the National Education Association (NEA) and the American Federation of Teachers (AFT). Prior to 1962 the NEA was a professional association of teachers, but in that year it began to act as a Wagner Act type union. The combined membership of NEA and AFT is plotted in Figure 4-1. Membership skyrocketed from 1962 to 1976. It has declined slightly since then. The Scholastic Aptitude Test (SAT) is the standard test administered nationwide to high school seniors and juniors who are college-bound. The SAT has two parts—math and verbal. The scores received by students on the SAT are also plotted in Figure 4-1. Those scores took a nosedive over the same years of the unions' most rapid growth. The rate of decline in the scores decreased as union membership began its slight decline. Of course, the close correlation depicted in Figure 4-1 does not prove that the growth in teachers' union membership caused the SAT scores to decline, but it is consistent with that hypothesis. In April 1983 the National Commission on Excellence in Education gave an "F" to the nation's public schools. The teachers' unions immediately claimed the problem was that not enough money was being spent on public schools. Figure 4-1 suggests an alternative hypothesis.

Table 4-6: Public Sector Bargaining and Strikes
(October 1971 - December 1982)

States	Average Number of Strikes per 100,000 Public Workers per State
Nationwide per state average	3.5
38 states with compulsory bargaining laws	4.2
12 states with no compulsory bargaining laws	1.7

Source: *Government Union Critique*, Public Services Research Foundation, February 25, 1983, p. 4.

Figure 4-1

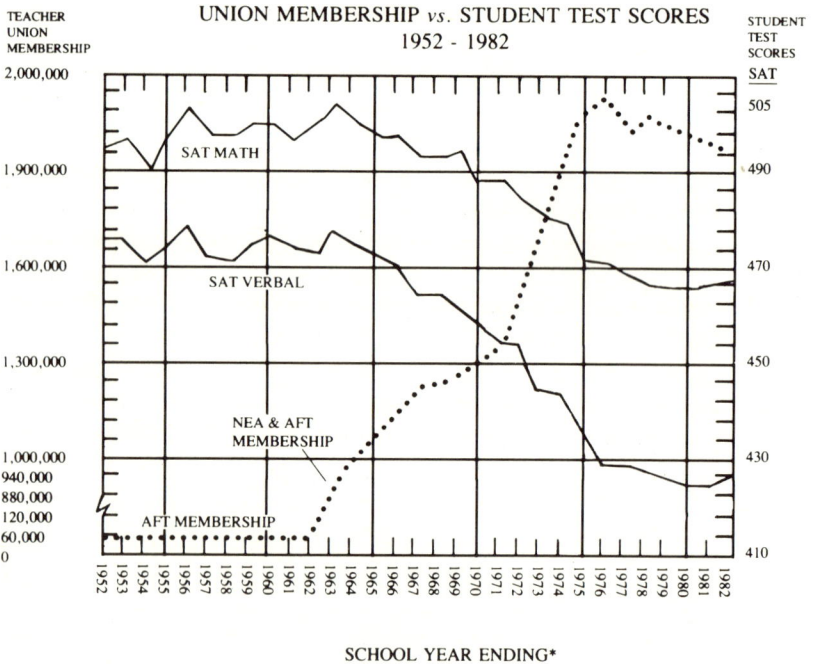

TEACHER UNION MEMBERSHIP

UNION MEMBERSHIP *vs.* STUDENT TEST SCORES
1952 - 1982

STUDENT TEST SCORES

SAT MATH

SAT VERBAL

NEA & AFT MEMBERSHIP

AFT MEMBERSHIP

SCHOOL YEAR ENDING*

*Teacher union membership figures based on calendar year

Source: *Government Union Critique*, Public Services Research Foundation, June 3, 1983, p. 5.

The record of peace in public sector labor relations is no different for public employees as a whole than it is for public school teachers. Table 4-6 shows the average number of strikes per 100,000 public workers per state from October 1971 to December 1982. There are 150% more strikes per 100,000 government workers in the thrity-eight states with compulsory bargaining laws than there are in the twelve states without compulsory bargaining laws. The message is clear: If we are to have peaceful labor relations in the public sector, all of the compulsory bargaining laws now in effect must be repealed. In those states where new or more severe compulsory bargaining laws are being considered for adoption, those opposed to such legislation should not let the unionists continue to get away with selling compulsion in the name of the pursuit of peaceful labor relations.

Productivity and Resource Mobility

Labor unions are cartels of sellers of labor services. They exist specifically to eliminate competition in labor markets. Sometimes the elimination of competition becomes as ludicrous as it is inefficient. Unions of craft workers are usually organized along craft lines—e.g., there is a union for electricians, another union for painters, one for carpenters, for bricklayers, for plumbers, for sheet metal workers, etc. In order to guard their individual turfs, these unions impose work rules on construction sites that greatly increase construction costs and expand the time necessary to complete any project. An electrician cannot move a ladder, for that is the province of a carpenter or a painter. A painter cannot unplug an extension cord, for that is the turf of the electrician. An electrician cannot tape and texture the sheetrock into which he has cut a space for an electrical outlet, for that is the job of tape-and-texture technicians. The stories are legion and humorous, but they are also, tragic. Workers stand around on construction sites doing nothing until work has been brought to the stage where they do their thing. All the while these workers collect full-time pay. The great difference between the costs of construction done by unionized firms and nonunionized firms is almost all accounted for by such oppressive union work rules.

Craft unions are, also, notorious for resisting technological changes that reduce production costs. The electricians' unions effectively delayed the introduction of Romex into the wiring of residential and commercial buildings. Romex is very easy to handle and install, and it is just as safe as the older metal-sheathed wiring, but the metal-sheathed wiring requires more time and labor to install. The painters' union successfully resisted the use of rollers instead of brushes for a long time. After it finally accepted rollers, it resisted spray guns. The plumbers' union first resisted copper pipe and solder in place of the standard screw-together steel pipe, and then it resisted the use of plastic pipes. Firemen on railroad locomotive engines resisted the introduction of diesel locomotives, and then when most railroads finally adopted the diesels the firemen insisted that their members accompany each diesel and get paid for doing nothing.

Both craft and industrial unions alike are notorious for penalizing workers who do their jobs too quickly and too well. "Beating the rate" causes employers to change their expectations about how much work can be done. And besides that, an outstanding worker is not maintaining his "solidarity" with his brothers and sisters. Workers who excel are "sent to Coventry" (ostracized). Merit pay for exceptionally good work is always resisted by union officers. They try to depict such payments as "elitist." They promote the idea that each worker is the same as every other worker, and what any worker is paid all workers must be paid. Unions similarly insist that layoffs be governed by seniority rather than productivity. Individual merit is quashed in favor of collectivist uniformity.

Unions that are successful in claiming for their members larger incomes than they otherwise would get face competition from nonunionized workers and foreign workers. In order to quash this competition unions lobby in favor of increases in minimum wage rates, Davis-Bacon type laws, and tariffs and import quotas. As a result all consumers and most workers suffer.

Both the federal government and the individual state governments set legal minimum wage rates. The current federal legal minimum wage is $3.35 per hour. Unionists who lobby in favor of such laws claim that they are concerned about the poor. It is more likely that they are attempting to increase the demand for unionized labor. Suppose there were two types of cars—Chevrolets and Cadillacs. If a law were passed that set a minimum price of $12,000 for Chevrolets, the demand for Cadillacs would increase. Some people are willing to buy Chevrolets instead of Cadillacs because of the substantial price difference. But if that price difference is narrowed, Cadillacs become relatively more attractive. It is the same for labor. Unionized labor tends to be skilled. Employers are willing to hire unskilled labor and use relatively simple machinery when wages paid to unskilled workers are sufficiently low. When a law is passed that narrows the wage gap between unskilled and skilled labor, the demand for the latter increases. It's an old rule: Prevent the competition from competing.

The Davis-Bacon Act forces contractors who work on federal construction projects to pay the "prevailing" wage for each type of labor. In practice this has always meant the union wage must be paid. Thus, in effect, nonunion firms are prevented from getting federal construction projects. A nonunion firm that pays lower wages than a union firm pays is prevented from even bidding on a federal project. This is another applicaion of the same old rule: Prevent the competition from competing.

Foreign suppliers of goods and services, and the workers who are employed thereby, are competitors of American unions. American consumers want to get whatever quality of product they desire at the lowest possible price. If union wages and work rules mean that American suppliers are high priced, American consumers will naturally turn to foreign suppliers. Unionists try to prevent consumers from protecting themselves in that way by lobbying to get Congress to add tariffs on to the prices of foreign goods and to limit the quantity of foreign goods that American consumers are allowed to purchase. Unionists claim they do this to protect American jobs. In fact, they are trying to protect their own jobs at the expense of other American jobs as well as American consumers. Foreigners pay for what we export to them with what they export to us. If we limit their exports to us, we limit their demand for our exports; and we, thus, decrease jobs in those export industries. This is another application of the same old rule: Prevent the competition from competing.

All successful attempts to prevent the competition from competing result in lower productivity. To get the most out of scarce resources it is necessary always to accomplish each task, produce each product and service, at the lowest possible cost. When consumers and employers are forced, through pro-unionist legislation to do things in the most costly way, rather than the least costly way, maximum production from available resources is not achieved.

Patterns of demand and supply are constantly changing in any healthy economy. Tomorrow probably will not look exactly like today. For people to get the most out of available resources, it is imperative that those resources be redeployed to keep up with the constantly changing patterns of demand and supply. The entrepreneurial, competitive market process described in Chapter 1 depends on the mobility of resources—capital and labor. If entrepreneurs cannot close up existing unprofitable or declining plants and open new ones, or decrease operations at some plants and increase operations at others, in response to changing economic opportunities and the market signals those opportunitites generate, the economy will gradually stagnate and run down. All of us will share in increasing poverty. Evidence to support this contention is obtained by comparing the average per capita incomes in countries where government decides where and how capital is invested and in countries where people are free to move resources in pursuit of private gain. A comparison of East Germany with West Germany, for example, would illustrate the point.

The NLRA has been used to prevent employers from closing down unprofitable plants and plants whose long-run profitability was declining. It has also been used to prevent decreases in operations, such as discontinuation of a product line and contracting out at single plants.

Section 8(a)(3) of the NLRA makes it an unfair labor practice for an employer to discourage union membership. In *Textile Workers Union of America v. Darlington Manufacturing Company* [267 U.S. 37 (1965)] the Supreme Court prevented an employer from shutting down a plant that had recently been unionized while it continued to operate plants that were not unionized. The Court held that such an action amounted to anti-union disrimination. The employer acted, the Court declared, with "anti-union animus." The Court held that the employer has an absolute right to shut down all plants together, but to shut down a unionized plant while continuing to operate nonunion plants because of "anti-union animus" was illegal. Ever since then whenever an employer wants to shut down a unionized plant he must be very careful that it is done in such a way that a Section 8(a)(3) violation cannot be sustained.[6]

Section 8(a)(5) of the NLRA makes it an unfair labor practice for an employer to refuse to bargain with a union that has achieved exclusive bargaining agent status. In *Fibreboard Paper Products Corp. v. NLRB* [379 U.S. 203 (1964)] the Court used this Section to force a company to engage in "decision bargaining" with the exclusive bargaining agent. After its existing contract with the union representing its maintenance workers expired, the compnay contracted-out its maintenance operations. The Court said that since the jobs of union workers were thereby eliminated the company could not reach such a decision without bargaining with the union. Since then other courts have used *Fibreboard* to declare that although decisions involving substantial amounts of investment capital or a basic change in the nature of the employer's business are the exclusive province of management to make, decisions involving such things as subcontracting, contracting-out, automation and consolidations of operations that eliminated union jobs must be made through "decision bargaining" with unions.[7]

Since labor law effectively restricts closures of only unionized plants, unions have pushed to get such laws as the 1979 National Employment Priorities Act, which would restrict plant closures in nonunionized as well as unionized plants, enacted. Unions recognize that if nonunionized plants are left free to close, capital will migrate to the nonunionized sector of the economy and union jobs will eventually substantially decline. Thus, a federal law that would take that advantage away from nonunionized plants is a highly valued goal of labor unions. This is yet another application of the same old rule: Prevent the competition from competing.

Unions and Inflation

Inflation is a sustained increase of the average level of money prices. The two most common measures of the average level of money prices are the Consumer Price Index and the Implicit Gross National Product Deflator. By either measure there was a severe inflation in the United States from the mid-1960s, throughout the 1970s, and at least until 1983. The current annual inflation rate—that rate at which the purchasing power of each dollar declines—is approximately 4%. When compared to the double-digit rates of the 1970s, that seems like a bit of good fortune. However, by longer-run historical standards, even 4% is an excessively high rate of inflation.

It is quite common for people to put a lot of blame on unions for the inflation. The common view is that unions raise wages and then employers have to raise prices in order to recoup the higher labor costs, but that view is quite mistaken. Unions do deserve a great deal of blame for inflation, but the connection between unions and inflation is much more subtle than this "wage-push-on-prices" thesis indicates and so many people believe.

If the amount of money in circulation relative to the quantity of goods and services that money is used to buy stays constant, then union-caused wage increases could not possibly cause inflation. If some wages are artificially raised by union strike-threat, some other wages are going to have to fall to make up the difference. Suppose that a union wage settlement causes the price of steel to go up. With no extra money in circulation, more money spent on steel has to mean that less money will be spent on other things. When less of those other things are bought there will be production cutbacks and layoffs in connection with the manufacture of those other things. Production cutbacks and layoffs put downward pressure on prices and wages in those employments. The price of steel could be higher, but the prices of some other things must, then, be lower. If the total dollar value of expenditures is fixed (as it is with a fixed money supply), higher prices somewhere have to result in lower prices elsewhere. There cannot be a general, sustained increase of the average level of prices.

Then where does inflation come from? It comes from an increase of the amount of money in circulation relative to the quantity of goods and services that the money is used to buy. Inflation is a fall in the purchasing power of the dollar. The dollar loses value—i.e., it loses its ability to buy other things. How many of other things could a picture of Mona Lisa buy if Da Vinci had painted 100 Mona Lisas? Surely the purchasing power of one Mona Lisa, then, would be less than the purchasing power of the one actual Mona Lisa that does exist. When the quantity of Mona Lisas increase relative to the quantity of the goods and services that a Mona Lisa could be used to buy, the value of any one Mona Lisa—its market exchange rate—will decline. It's exactly the same with pictures of George Washington. A necessary and sufficient condition for inflation to occur is the creation of new money at a pace faster than the creation of additional goods and services for which the money is destined to be exchanged.

Now unions do not create new money. Only the government, through the Federal Reserve System, has the ability to create new money and put it into circulation. What, then, are the connections between unions and inflation?

There are two connections—a supply side connection and a demand side connection.[8] The crucial variable is the amount of money in circulation relative to the supply of goods and services on which the money is spent. On the supply side, through their restrictive work rules and interferences with resource mobility, unions make the supply of goods and services available to be purchased by consumers smaller than it otherwise would be. Moreover, union advocacy of increases of the legal minimum wage and such measures as the Davis-Bacon Act diminish employment opportunities for many workers and, thus, decrease the supply of goods and services to be bought. These supply reductions mean that for any given rate of increase of the money supply the concomitant inflation rate will be higher than it otherwise would be.

On the demand side unions lobby for government spending programs that create deficits. When the government spends more money than it takes in through taxation it usually, in effect, prints up new money with which to carry out its spending plans. Nominally, the federal government makes up the revenue shortfall by borrowing money from the private sector. But, in order to avoid higher interest rates that are likely to occur when the government actively competes for loan funds in the private credit markets, the Federal Reserve System (the Fed) buys government securities from the private credit market. The Fed pays for the securities it buys with checks that are not drawn against any account whatsoever. It buys them, in other words, with newly created money.[9] Thus, to the extent that advocacy by unions of government spending plans results in deficits that are larger than they otherwise would be, such advocacy results in increases in the creation of new money. For any given rate of growth of the supply of goods and sevices available to be bought with money, the resulting inflation rate will be higher than it otherwise would be.

There are many examples of union advocacy of increasing federal expenditures. The Davis-Bacon Act makes federal expenditures on construction projects higher than they otherwise would be. Union advocacy of public assistance programs, most of which are needed only because of the disemployment effects of such things as legal minimum wages, adds to the problem. Union advocacy of federally-funded job programs, which again are only necessary because of the disemployment effects of legal minimum wages and other union-backed government interventions in labor markets, also contributes substantially to deficits. George Meany made clear the extent of union culpability for inflation when he said, in 1978, "Every piece of social welfare legislation in the last two decades carries a union label...."[10]

The only effective way to reduce the ability of unions to influence public spending and impair productivity is to repeal all those laws that give them powers of coercion. If unions were wholly voluntary associations with no more or no less power than other voluntary organizations, inflation would be less of a problem than it has been in the recent past and still is today.

The Solution

Government regulation of economic activities has recently lost some of its appeal. Beginning in the mid-1960s and throughout the 1970s the amount and scope of government regulation expanded tremendously. But by the end of the 1970s it was becoming clear to many people that government regulatory actions made the problems to which they were addressed worse rather than better. Deregulation vs. regulation was a major issue of the Congressional and Presidential campaigns of 1980, and those advocating deregulation won. The labor market is the most heavily regulated market of all. Although no politicians are overtly arguing in favor of deregulation of the labor market, such deregulation is the principal way that conditions for the average working person can be improved.

The labor market has been subjected to two kinds of government regulation—procedural and substantive.[11] Procedural regulations concern the permissible ways and means that employees and employers come together in the formation of hiring contracts. The NLRA is the primary federal procedural regulation. Substantive regulations define by government fiat the limits of permissible terms of trade between employees and employers. Such laws as the 1936 Fair Labor Standards Act, that empowers the federal government to set legal minimum wage rates and maximum working hours, and the 1970 Occupational Safety and Health Act, that mandates workplace safety and health rules, are examples of substantive regulations. The proposal I made at the beginning of this chapter—that the NLRA, the Norris-LaGuardia Act, the Railway Labor Act, and all state Wagner Act type legislation be repealed—is simply a call for the abolition of all procedural regulation of the labor market. (I also support substantive deregulation, but that is not the subject matter of this book.)

Who bears the cost of procedural labor market regulation? Most people. Consumers pay higher prices, taxpayers pay higher taxes, and many employees and employers pay the costs of compulsion and regimentation. Many employees even receive lower incomes than they otherwise would, and the overall health and vigor of the economy is impaired. *Who benefits from procedural regulation of the labor market? Very few.* Employees of the government agencies that carry out the procedural regulations (e.g., employees of the NLRB) benefit, for they are provided with jobs and job security that they would not otherwise have. If the NLRB were abolished those employees would have to seek alternative employment, and the employments they find may not be as attractive as the sinecures they now enjoy. Union officials also benefit for they derive their incomes from the dues that many workers are compelled to pay as a condition for maintaining their jobs. And politicians also benefit from compulsory labor unions; for such unions, fat with the wealth of forced collection of dues and fees, are highly-organized political pressure groups whose assistance at election time is highly valued. Any organization that can command the troops necessary to run get-out-the-vote drives, carpools, phone banks, and leaflet campaigns, is a valuable ally during any election effort.

The fact that the beneficiaries of the NLRA are relatively few in number and well organized and disciplined, while those who suffer from the regulation are many and unorganized means that it is almost politically impossible to abolish the NLRA. Even the Reagan administration recently demonstrated its fear of the political power of compulsory unions. In June 1983 Labor Secretary Ray Donovan ordered the U.S. Labor Department to withdraw a study that was done for the Department by Dr. Edwin Vieira, Jr. which showed that compulsory unions were probably guilty of violating the 1974 Employment Retirement Income Security Act in their administration of members' pension fund investments. While not addressing himself to the evidence, John H. Lyons, Chairman of the AFL-CIO Committee on Investment of Union Pension Funds, complained to Donovan that the Vieira study was "an anti-union diatribe and a waste of taxpayers' money."[12] Without argument, apparently with his eyes on the 1984 political campaign, Donovan complied with the union's demand that the study be suppressed.

Most members of Congress in both houses are also apparently afraid of the political clout of compulsory unions. During the 1960s several Southern states refused to protect the civil rights of Blacks. The federal government, quite rightly I believe, stepped in and provided Blacks with the protective and judicial services to which every citizen is entitled by natural law and the U.S. Constitution. However, when it comes to protecting citizens against acts of violence perpetrated by union activists against nonunion workers and employers, the federal government does nothing. Unionists claim that state and local law enforcement agencies are responsible for protecting people against violence, and the federal government is not needed. This is the same argument used by many Southerners during the 1960s. Senator Charles Grassley (R, IA) has introduced federal legislation which would empower federal law enforcement agencies to step in to situations of violence in labor disputes where state and local agencies have failed to do their jobs.[13] The dangers of allowing labor unions to be above the law are well illustrated in Great Britain. Since the Trade Disputes Act of 1906 labor unions in Britain have had complete legal immunity against tort actions. They have also enjoyed a *de facto* immunity against prosecution for overt acts of violence committed during labor disputes. The Grassley bill if adopted would go a long way toward forestalling the trend in America toward the kind of labor union privilege that has so damaged the British economy.[14]

Many of those politicians who are most vociferous in support of federal enforcement of civil rights for Blacks are just as vociferous in their condemnation of the Grassley proposal. They claim it is "anti-labor." In fact, it is not anti-labor at all. It is anti-violence. There are many more workers who are victimized by the violence than there are those who are benefitted by it.

In spite of the formidable political clout of compulsory unions, I believe it will be possible, perhaps in the not-so-distant future, to repeal the NLRA. Labor unions are becoming increasingly less popular with workers, at least in the private sector. Table 4-7 shows that compulsory unions are winning a declining percentage of representation elections, and they are losing a very high percentage of decertification elections. Even with all of the advantages of compulsion, more and more workers are escaping from domination by labor unions.

Table 4-7: Representation and Decertification Election Results 1956-1980

Year	Percent of Representation Elections Won by Unions	Percent of Decertification Elections Lost by Unions
1956	65.3%	68.9%
1966	60.8	74.4
1976	48.1	72.8
1977	46.0	76.0
1978	46.0	73.6
1979	45.0	75.0
1980	45.7	72.7

Source: *Annual Report* National Labor Relations Board, various years, Tables 13 and 17

The escape rate so alarmed unionists that they tried to get a "labor law reform" measure enacted into federal law in 1977. That "reform" would have given the unions even more powers of compulsion by speeding up the representation (but not decertification) election process while curtailing employers' freedom of speech during representation election campaigns, by enlarging and packing the NLRB with pro-union members, by providing that the larger NLRB could deny federal contracts to any employers that asked for court reviews of NLRB decisions, and by forcing such employers to pay Bureau of Labor Statistics index wage rates during the court review.[15] The measure passed the House of Representatives but did not make it through the Senate. Apparently, there is some limit to the political clout of compulsory unions.

If the NLRA were repealed, voluntarism would replace compulsion in American labor markets. Unions would become the voluntary organizations envisioned by Samuel Gompers. It is impossible to put a dollar figure on the psychic benefits people would gain from replacing compulsion with freedom of choice. However, one estimate has been made that the measurable economic benefits from repeal of the NLRA would be $22 billion annually.[16] This figure includes benefits from lower prices, lower taxes, reduced unemployment, increased productivity, easing of inflationary pressures, and the improvement of the competitive strength of American-made products. The labor market would no longer be beset with disputes over issues like fair representation (unions would represent only those people who freely chose to be so represented, thus no worker could claim the union wasn't meeting its legal responsibility to represent everyone fairly), and appropriate bargaining units (since bargaining would be voluntary there would be no need to determine legal bargaining units).

In Conclusion

On September 19, 1981 American unionism sponsored a "Solidarity Day" demonstration in Washington, D.C. In conducting such an affair the unions hoped to capture some of the goodwill that most Americans have for the independent Polish labor union, Solidarity. American unions frequently quote Pope John-Paul II's declaration that all workers have an "innate right" to form labor unions as support of their belief that all American workers ought (although they don't put it this way) to be forced to join American unions.

To confuse Solidarity with American unions is to discredit Solidarity. Solidarity is a wholly voluntary organization actively fighting against government oppression and in favor of individual rights. American unions are allied with a coercive government agency—the NLRB—to force American workers to give up their individual rights in favor of the collectivist "rights" of unions. As long as the NLRA is in force American unions cannot justly claim the moral high ground occupied by Solidarity.[17]

In May 1935 when the Wagner Act was debated in the Congress, Senator Millard E. Tydings from Maryland offered an amendment to Section 7 of the proposed bill. Tydings would have had that section read:

Employees shall have the right to self organization, to form, join, or assist labor organizations, to bargain collectively through representatives of their own choosing, and to engage in other concerted activities, for the purpose of collective bargaining or other mutual aid or protection, *free from coercion or intimidation from any source.*[18]

The italicized clause was Tydings' addition to the proposed Section 7. He was concerned that the Wagner Bill as proposed offered protection to workers from abuse by employers, but it offered no protection to workers against abuse by labor unions. A worker should, he felt, be free to join and support or *not* to join and support a union as he felt best. The Tydings amendment was rejected in the Senate by a vote of fifty to twenty-one. The Senate, in other words, seemed to suggest that some forms of private coercion are all right while others are not.

If the Congress repealed the NLRA now it would finally be asserting the sensible proposition that all forms of private coercion are reprehensible. No private group of individuals, whether a majority or a minority of employees on a job, could then force any other employees to accept the representation services of any labor union against their will. No majority or minority of employees could then force unwilling workers to pay dues or agency fees to any union against their will. Freed from the shackles of procedural regulation of the labor market, employers and employees together could experiment with alternative forms of labor-management relations procedures. Successful ones would be adopted and imitated, unsuccessful ones would be discarded. Entrepreneurial alertness to mutually beneficial innovation would enable American enterprise once again to become an effective international competitor. Clearly the game is worth the candle.

NOTES

1. Norman J. Simler, *The Impact of Unionism on Wage-Income Ratio in the Manufacturing Sector of the Economy* (Minneapolis: University of Minnesota Press, 1962).

2. Myron Lieberman, *Public-Sector Bargaining* (Lexington: Lexington Books, 1980), p. 2.

3. Robert A. Nisbet, "Public Unions and the Decline of Social Trust," in A. Lawrence Chickering, ed., *Public Employee Unions* (San Francisco: Institute of Contemporary Studies, 1976), p. 14.

4. Irving Bernstein, *The New Deal Collective Bargaining Policy* (Berkeley: University of California Press, 1950), p. 153.

5. *Government Union Critique*, Public Services Research Foundation, February 11, 1983), p. 5.

6. Richard McKenzie, *Fugitive Industry* (San Francisco: The Pacific Institute, 1984), Chapter 5.

7. *Ibid.*

8. Dwight R. Lee, *The Inflationary Impact of Labor Unions*, Center for Education and Research in Free Enterprise, Texas A & M University, Research Monograph Series, No. 5, 1980.

9. For a complete discussion of this money creation process see Charles W. Baird, *Elements of Macroeconomics*, second edition (St. Paul: West Publishing Co., 1981), Chapter 10.

10. Quoted in Dwight R. Lee, *op. cit.*, p. 16.

11. Dan C. Heldman, James T. Bennett, and Manuel H. Johnson, *Deregulating Labor Relations* (Dallas: The Fisher Institute, 1981), Chapter 3.

12. *Government Union Critique*, Public Services Research Foundation, July 1, 1983, p. 8.

13. *National Right to Work Newsletter*, National Right to Work Committee, June 30, 1983, p. 5.

14. I am grateful to P. J. White, Ian Sams, and Donald Rutherford from the University of Edinburgh for explaining the peculiarities of British labor law to me during my visit there in June 1983. For an excellent discussion of some of the lessons that Americans could learn from the British experience see John Burton, *The Political Future of American Trade Unions*, the Heritage Lectures 12, The Heritage Foundation, 1983.

15. For a thorough analysis of the proposed legislation see *Proposed Amendments to the National Labor Relations Act*, American Enterprise Institute Legislative Analysis No. 23, February 23, 1978.

16. Heldman, *et al.*, *op. cit.*, p. 121.

17. Charles W. Baird, "Polish Solidarity vs. American Unionism," *Government Union Review*, Winter 1982, pp. 47-57.

18. Bernstein, *op. cit.*, pp. 115-16.